C. S. Lewis:
The Man and His Achievement

C. S. Lewis:
The Man and
His Achievement

JOHN PETERS

Exeter
The Paternoster Press

AUSTRALIA
Bookhouse and Australia Ltd.,
P. O. Box 115, Flemington Markets, NSW 2129

SOUTH AFRICA
Oxford University Press,
P. O. Box 1141, Cape Town

British Library Cataloguing in Publication Data
Peters, John
    C. S. Lewis – the man and his achievement.
    1.   Lewis, C. S.——Criticism and interpretation
    I.   Title
    828'.91209   PR6023.E926Z/

ISBN 0-85364-365-2

Typset in Great Britain by
Photo·Graphics, 184 High Street, Honiton, Devon
and printed for The Paternoster Press,
Paternoster House, 3 Mount Radford Cresent, Exeter, Devon
by A. Wheaton & Co. Ltd., Exeter, Devon.

Contents

Acknowledgements

The copyright material listed below is reprinted by kind permission of the following:

Collins (William) Sons & Co.
Christian Reflections, Fernseed and Elephants, The Four Loves, The Great Divorce, The Letters of C. S. Lewis (W. H. Lewis Ed.) Letters to Malcolm, Mere Christianity, Miracles, The Pilgrim's Regress, The Problem of Pain, Reflections on the Psalms, The Screwtape Letters, Screwtape Proposes a Toast, Surprised by Joy, They Stand Together (Walter Hooper Ed.) Till We Have Faces.

Wm. B. Eerdmans
Letters to an American Lady

Hodder & Stoughton
A Severe Mercy (Sheldon Vanauken)
Born Again (Charles W. Colson)

Oxford University Press
A Preface to Paradise Lost
English Literature in the Sixteenth Century

Faber & Faber
A Grief Observed (T. S. Eliot)
East Coker (T. S. Eliot)

Routledge & Kegan Paul
Milton Criticism (James Thorpe Ed.)

The Bodley Head
Out of the Silent Planet
That Hideous Strength

George Allen & Unwin
J. R. R. Tolkien: A Biography (Humphrey Carpenter)

Macmillan Publishers
Sprightly Running (John Wain)

CHAPTER ONE

An Abiding Influence

C. S. Lewis died – as did President Kennedy – on the afternoon of Friday 22nd November 1963, just a week before his sixty-fifth birthday. Unlike the smitten American politician, he did so in the familiar and peaceful surroundings of his own home, 'The Kilns', in Oxford. Since September 1961 he had been in essence an invalid, with all the restrictions and annoying difficulties which that term implies, and he had clearly accepted the encroachment of death but said nothing to his friends. Writing to an American correspondent on 28th June 1963, he advised her to think of herself as a seed embedded patiently in the earth and waiting 'to come up a flower in the Gardener's good time, up into the *real* world, the real waking', and he added, 'I suppose that our whole present life, looked back on from there, will seem only a drowsy half-waking. We are here in the land of dreams. But cock-crow is coming.' Tranquil assurance, then, in the face of death marked his final days, in spite of much suffering. For three weeks in July 1963 he was a patient in the Acland Nursing Home. He received Extreme Unction at 2 p.m. on 16th July (administered by Father Michael Watts of St Mary Magdalene's), but after a distressing period of dreams and 'tangled reason' he was allowed home, accompanied by a nurse. His last letter to his life-long friend Arthur Greeves, dated 11th September 1963, expressed his regret that he had revived in July but he declared that he was not unhappy.[3] In August he felt constrained to resign his Chair and Fellowship at Cambridge and was then made an honorary Fellow of Magdalene. Upon receiving this honour Lewis wrote urbanely to the Master, Sir Henry Willink,[4] saying that his ghost would haunt the place whence the most appreciated of his honours had come. He had been enormously happy and reposed at Magdalene and referred revealingly, in the same letter, to the close and domestic bond which had bound him to that famous college. A little less than a month later 'Time's winged chariot' bore him away,[5] and the term was indeed over for one of the most brilliant scholars and stimulating Christian apologists of the twentieth-century. His had been a life-time of ceaseless endeavour: of writing, lecturing, debating, broadcasting and, not least, of corresponding with people all over the world on literary, religious and personal matters. A giant had been taken from the battle and in the realm of Christian apologetics he has had no successor.

Lewis's reputation rests not only on his numerous publications, but also on the immediate impact of his larger-than-life personality. It would not be inappropriate to apply the epithets 'formidable' and 'dynamic' to him. This was precisely the impression he made on an American, Sheldon Vanauken, who encountered Lewis in Oxford during the nineteen-fifties: 'What I met, when I turned up at his rooms, was John Bull himself. Portly, jolly, a wonderful grin, a big voice, a quizzical gaze—and no nonsense. ... Withal the most genial of companions.'[6]

Following this meeting with Lewis, Vanauken and Davy, his wife, embarked on a study of Christianity. They began by reading *Miracles*, *The Screwtape Letters*, and the science-fiction trilogy (*Out of the Silent Planet*, *Perelandra* and *That Hideous Strength*) which showed them that 'the Christian God might, after all, be quite big enough for the whole galaxy'.[7] Other influences included G. K. Chesterton and T. S. Eliot, but overwhelmingly their most important reading was Lewis. Vanauken felt that if 'minds like St Augustine's and Newman's and Lewis's could wrestle with Christianity and become fortresses of that faith, it had to be taken seriously.'

The next stage was the beginning of a correspondence with Lewis, in which Vanauken expressed his fundamental dilemma:

I can't believe in Christ unless I have faith, I can't have faith unless I believe in Christ. This is 'the leap.' If to *be* a Christian is to have faith (and clearly it is), I can put it thus: I must accept Christ to become a Christian, but I must *be* a Christian to accept Him. I don't have faith and I don't as yet believe, but everyone seems to say: 'You must have faith to believe.' Where do I get it? Or will you tell me something different? Is there a proof? Can Reason carry one over the gulf ... without faith?

Why does God expect so much of us? Why does He require this effort to believe? If He made it clear that He is – as clear as a sunrise or a rock or a baby's cry – wouldn't we be right joyous to choose Him and His Law? Why should the right exercise of our free will contain this fear of intellectual dishonesty?[8]

Lewis replied promptly:

The contradiction 'we must have faith to believe and must believe to have faith' belongs to the same class as those by which the Eleatic philosophers proved that all motion was impossible. And there are many others. You can't swim unless you can support yourself in water & you can't support yourself in water unless you can swim. Or again, in an act of volition (e.g. getting up in the morning) is the very beginning of the act itself voluntary or involuntary? If voluntary, then you must have willed it, ∴ it was not really the beginning. If involuntary, then the continuation of the act (being determined by the first moment) is involuntary too. But in spite of this we *do* swim, & we *do* get out of bed.[9]

Gradually, aided by Lewis's probings, their attitude to Christianity underwent a transformation.

Christianity now appeared intellectually stimulating and aesthetically exciting. The personality of Jesus emerged from the Gospels with astonishing consistency. Whenever they were written, they were written in the shadow of a personality so

tremendous that Christians who may never have seen him knew
him utterly: that strange mixture of unbearable sternness and
heartbreaking tenderness. No longer did the Church appear
only a disreputable congeries of quarrelling sects: now we saw
the Church, splendid and terrible, sweeping down the centuries
with anthems and shining crosses and steady-eyed saints. No
longer was the Faith something for children: intelligent people
held it strongly – and they walked to a secret singing that we
could not hear. Or *did* we hear something: high and clear and
unbearably sweet?

Christianity had come to seem to us *probable*. It all hinged on
this Jesus. Was he, in fact, the Lord Messiah, the Holy One of
Israel, the Christ? Was he, indeed, the incarnate God? Very God
of very God? This was the heart of the matter. *Did* he rise from
the dead? The Apostles, the Evangelists, Paul believed it with
utter conviction. Could we believe on their belief? Believe in a
miracle? The fact that we had never seen a miracle did not prove,
or even imply, that there might not be miracles at the supreme
occasion of history. There was absolutely no proof, no proof
possible, that it didn't happen. No absolute proof that it did. It
seemed to us probable. It had a sort of *feel* of truth. A ring of
truth. But was that enough?[10]

Later both Sheldon and Davy took the leap of faith and
committed themselves to Jesus Christ. The last six lines of
Sheldon's sonnet expressed their response:

Between the probable and proved there yawns
A gap. Afraid to jump, we stand absurd,
Then see *behind* us sink the ground and, worse,
Our very standpoint crumbling. Desperate dawns
Our only hope: to leap into the Word
That opens up the shuttered universe.[11]

Significantly and typically, Lewis's part in this process had
been both personal and literary. He had given the two
searching Americans lucid, straightforward, logical and imaginative answers to their queries, had prayed for them, and
generally taken a keen interest in their progress and developing understanding of Christian affairs. Later still a
friendship began between Sheldon and Lewis; they were to
become 'companions in distress' as each lost his wife after a
painful illness. Their last meeting occurred only a fortnight
before Lewis's death.

Because his was such a strong personality, many wondered whether Lewis's influence would simply fade away after his death. Happily this has not occurred to any great extent simply because his books continue to be sold in huge quantities both in Britain and in America. A notable illustration of his abiding influence is found in Charles Colson's book, *Born Again*, which was published in 1976.[12] Described by *Time* magazine as 'tough, wily, nasty and tenaciously loyal to Richard Nixon', Colson rose to a position of eminence and power under a president noted for his ruthlessness, trickery and manipulation of the democratic processes. Thus it was that a hard-boiled Washington reacted with astonishment when Colson announced that he had undergone a religious conversion, and not a few suspected that the dramatic headline, 'Colson makes a decision for Christ', was yet another political gimmick by an astute manipulator. Incredulity was rife, but as it turned out there was no deception; the change in Colson was both impressive and convincing to his family, friends and professional partners. The story is significant, because a vitally important element in the process leading to his radical and thorough-going conversion to Christianity was Lewis's *Mere Christianity*, which had been given to Colson by a friend. While reading the chapter on 'The Great Sin' he felt 'naked and unclean', his 'bravado defences gone'. His graphic and eloquent description deserves to be quoted in full.

'Now sitting in the dimly lit porch, my self-centred past was washing over me in waves. It was painful. Agony. Desperately I tried to defend myself. ... The truth, I saw in an instant, was that I had wanted the position in the White House more than I had wanted money. There was no sacrifice. And the more I had talked about my own sacrifices, the more I was really trying to build myself up in the eyes of others. I would eagerly have given up everything I'd ever earned to prove myself at the mountain of government. It was pride – Lewis's great sin – that had propelled me through life.[13]

Colson found that Lewis's comments on pride had shattered him completely, not least because he was facing an intellect that was 'disciplined', 'lucid', and 'relentlessly logical'. He was honest enough to admit that Lewis's statement – 'The moment you have a self at all, there is the possibility of putting yourself first – wanting to be the centre – wanting to be God' – was a penetrating and damning indictment of his entire life, and especially of his political ambitions and activities. Self-assertion, willingness to trample on the lives and hopes of other people without caring a fig about them, all these things had to be jettisoned completely, and they were. *Mere Christianity* ultimately proved an extremely powerful, perhaps even irresistible, influence among those which led this rugged – and invariably ruthless – man to a definite Christian faith and certainty. What so disconcerted and also impressed Colson was Lewis's particular brand of inexorable logic, that special dialectical skill first shown by him at Great Bookham under his tutor W. T. Kirkpatrick, and his ability to expose cant and hypocrisy with a few carefully chosen words. Purely emotional arguments would have left Colson coldly unimpressed and would have been summarily dismissed. Colson's legal training and intuitive intelligence made him a redoubtable opponent for all but the sharpest of intelligences, which is precisely what he encountered in the former Oxford and Cambridge scholar, whose formidable powers of reasoning, allied to his firm and clear grasp of biblical truths, compelled respect from the former presidential aide. An inevitable side-effect of Colson's revelations was the elevation of *Mere Christianity* to the top of America's best-seller lists.

In numerous other ways, too, Lewis's name has been kept in the minds of British and American readers. Mainly instrumental in this is Walter Hooper who has edited a substantial number of his works, including *Christian Reflections* (1967), *Selected Literary Essays* (1969), *Undeceptions: Essays on Theology and Ethics* (1971), as well as collaborating with Roger Lancelyn Green in writing the official *Biography* (1974). More recently Hooper has brought out a magisterial edition of the letters which passed between Lewis and his life-long Irish friend, Arthur Greeves, *They Stand Together* (1979). The publication of this last volume, together with two other volumes of his letters,[14] have further revealed Lewis's personality and mind, as have such works as *Light on C. S. Lewis* (1965), *The Christian World of C. S. Lewis* (1965) and *A Mind Awake* (1968), the last two edited by Professor Clyde Kilby, the first one by Jocelyn Gibb.

Other writers have offered hagiography or personal reminiscences and there has been a profusion of 'guides' to his thought (for example, Simmons' guide to the 'Narnia Chronicles')[15] or 'keys' to his symbolism. Consider also the yearly sales of his books and the efforts of such magazines as 'The New York C. S. Lewis Society' and 'The Canadian C. S. Lewis Society', and it is not difficult to believe that Lewis, though dead, yet lives and speaks.

In all this profusion, however, some writers have tended to present naïve and inaccurate pictures of the man and his work, or have been decidedly trivial in their approach. One might be tempted to say that with some of his friends and admirers he has no need of enemies! Equally unacceptable is that form of cynicism that persuades publishers to link their works with Lewis's name in order to boost their sales and output (often in the most artificial way), while occasionally a title is adopted for a book (e.g. *Sustained By Joy*,[16] a republished series of sermons on Philippians) which has a verbal link with Lewis's work intended to attract the public's attention. Where Lewis's thinking is conveniently fitted into a pre-conceived mould, the result is a distortion of his views, an unfair reflection of what he said, and thus an undervaluing of his real quality and worth.

What is needed now is a cool and sober re-assessment of his intrinsic value and interest for a world twenty years on from his death. Such an agenda does not mean that this book is a debunking exercise. Its basic assumption is that Lewis has something of real value to say to a world that is divided politically, socially, ethically and ideologically, and is even more cynical and hard-boiled than it was when Lewis was alive. Its other assumption is that his reputation can best be served by a fair and rational approach to his life and work. Indeed much of the frippery which has been published about him would, if he were alive, earn his firm rebuke. It seems equally important to stress that he was not a Christian who *happened* to write on literary and scholarly matters, but someone with a first-rate mind who also took seriously the doctrines of the Bible and who sought to communicate his faith in a lively, logical, and imaginative way. Having said all this, it must be added that far greater expertise than mine would be needed to undertake the lengthy and detailed re-examination of his works required in order to assess their true significance. This work is by an ordinary person for ordinary people, with the fervent hope that it will lead them to read or re-read Lewis's works. Evaluation or literary criticism can never take the place of the original itself. Readers should, therefore, view this book as a *personal response* to certain aspects of Lewis's great output; in particular it will make extensive use of his letters, which have so far not received a detailed treatment.

My chosen method has been to allow Lewis to speak for himself as much as possible; he is by far the best and ablest commentator on and elucidator of his works, and this is where his letters act as companion volumes to his published works and help to substantiate certain of his attitudes or beliefs. In *Mere Christianity*, for example, he makes the forthright claim that in those lectures he is making a statement about the *essence* of Christianity, at the centre of which is the undeniable obligation to forgive those who may have sinned against or offended us in some way, the corollary being that to refuse to forgive others leads to our being refused forgiveness in turn. When we turn to one of his letters,[17] we find that only towards the end of his life was he able to forgive the cruel schoolmaster who had made his life as a child so unhappy. Lewis had made many attempts to do so before, but failed right until he was on the point of death.

Lewis's letters also give first-hand evidence about his life which his biographers have been able to draw on quite extensively. They indicate that his closing days *were* peaceful and that he faced his end with courage and dignity. On 25th June 1963, he writes to Mary, the American lady whose correspondence with him lasted for thirteen years and who at times must have been a considerable burden to him:

> Tho' horrified at your sufferings, I am overjoyed at the blessed change in your attitude to death. This is a bigger stride forward than perhaps you yourself yet know. For you *were* rather badly

wrong on that subject. Only a few months ago when I said that we old people hadn't much more to do than to make a good exit, you were almost angry with me for what you called such a "bitter" remark. Thank God, you now see it wasn't bitter; only plain common sense. Yes: I do wonder why the doctors inflict such torture to delay what cannot in any case be very long delayed. Or why God does! Unless there is still something for you to do, as far as weakness allows. I hope, now that you know you are forgiven, you will spend most of your remaining strength in *forgiving*. Lay all the old resentments down at the wounded feet of Christ. I have had dozens of blood transfusions in the last two years and know only too well the horrid — and *long* — moments during which they are poking about to find the vein. And then you think they've really got in at last and it turns out that they haven't. (Is there an allegory here? The approaches of Grace often hurt because the spiritual vein in us hides itself from the celestial surgeon?). But oh, I do pity you for waking up and finding yourself still on the wrong side of the door! How awful it must have been for poor Lazarus who had actually died, got it all over, and then was brought back — to go through it all, I suppose, a few years later. I think he, not St. Stephen, ought really to be celebrated as the first martyr.[18]

To Miss Jane Douglas he wrote on 27th October 1963, remarking that autumn was the best of the four seasons and adding: 'I'm not sure that old age isn't the best part of life. But of course, like autumn, it doesn't *last*.'[19] Less than a month later he was on the 'right' side of the door. Quite a large part of this work is devoted to a consideration of Lewis's apologetic output, which is exactly that aspect of his life and work which I have found most encouraging and strengthening. I hope that reading this volume may stimulate some people to look again at such works as *Mere Christianity* and lead others to explore them for the first time.

CHAPTER TWO

A Sketch of Lewis's Life

Somebody once asked Lewis for his views on the hydrogen bomb. Having thought about the subject for a while, he pointed out that the painful end of the world had been expected since the eleventh century at least, adding, 'Anyhow, when the bomb falls there will always be just that split second in which one can say, "Pooh! you're only a bomb. I'm an immortal soul."' On this joke the late Professor Coghill commented: 'Ulster, Greece, Rome, Oxford and Cambridge were in that joke.'[1] The words provide a convenient starting-point for an account of Lewis's life.

Schoolboy and Student

Coghill's reference to Ulster serves as a reminder that Lewis was born in Belfast on 29th November 1898, the second son of Albert and Flora Lewis. He was one of two children and his brother Warren had been born three years previously on 16th June 1895. They were to remain close and intimate – though not always harmonious – friends throughout their lives, and Warren was with his brother when he died almost sixty-five years later. Lewis tells us that there were two main elements in the family background, both radically different and mutually contradictory. On his father's side there was an abundance of rhetoric, passion and sentiment, with much alternating of mood between anger, laughter and sadness, and tenderness. He felt, rightly perhaps, that the Welsh have not 'much of the talent for happiness'. On his mother's side there was a rational and critical awareness, with a distinct 'talent for happiness in a high degree'.[2] Right from the start of his life, therefore, he experienced this dichotomy as well as other paradoxes existing in the fabric of the family.

The temperamental differences between his parents – his mother's consistently cheerful affection on the one hand, his father's emotional changes on the other – were demonstrated in other ways too. His mother was an avid reader of substantial novels, for example by Meredith or Tolstoy, while his father preferred political authors like Trollope. But neither was interested in the sort of romantic poetry or feeling which claimed Lewis's fervent allegiance from the very moment he began to choose books for himself. A glimpse into his childhood is given early on in *An Experiment in Criticism* where he refers to families who regard reading as a 'status symbol', and who are 'entirely dominated by fashion'.[3] As opposed to all this, there is the genuine literary experience of the boy reading a classic like *Treasure Island* under the bed-clothes and by the light of a torch. Clearly Lewis came into the latter category.

Lewis sums up the events of his childhood as 'not in the least other worldly', not 'even imaginative', and the whole period survives in his memory as one of 'humdrum, prosaic happiness',[4] evoking no particular nostalgia. It was not an especially happy childhood, therefore, but there were several bright lights burning on his horizon. One was the warm relationship with his brother (already alluded to) with whom he was truly a confederate and an ally from the first. Another was the fact that between the formative ages of six and eight he lived almost entirely in his own imagination.[5] Three aspects of this romantic landscape are worth recalling. The first is, in reality, a memory concerning a memory, when momentarily, as he stood by a flowering currant bush on a summer day, he was consumed by a sensation 'of desire'. The second was the book, *Squirrel Nutkin*, to which he returned frequently because he was troubled by the 'Idea

of Autumn', a glimpse into another dimension altogether.
The third came to him through poetry: he happened to be
reading the unrhymed translation of *Tegner's Drapa* one day
when, with sickening intensity, he was 'uplifed into the
huge regions of the northern sky', compared with which
ordinary life seems 'flat, stale, and profitless'.

This period was highly significant in his experience for it
brought him a sense of indefinable longing (*Sehnsucht*), that
unsatisfied desire which John feels with such incredible
force in *The Pilgrim's Regress*, and which is so very different
from ordinary feelings of grief or sadness, pleasure or fun.[6]
In all probability such an emotional retreat and release was
all the more necessary because his relationship with his
father was always uneasy, indeed frequently difficult, and
the effect of Flora's premature death from cancer, on 23rd
August 1908, was to distance the boys further from their
father. In fact though, as Lewis admits in *Surprised by Joy*,
the 'real bereavement' had taken place even before his
mother's death, and the time leading up to it was almost
unbearable, for the brothers were, in Lewis's graphic
phrase, 'two frightened urchins huddled together for
warmth in a bleak world.'[7]

The next stage – being sent away to a boarding school –
was inevitable, but this did nothing to diminish Lewis's
great feeling of unhappiness at this time, and he later
referred to Wynyard School in Hertfordshire as 'Belsen',
while the chapter in *Surprised by Joy* describing his life
there, between the ages of ten and twelve, is headed simply
and derisively, 'Concentration Camp'. His distaste for this
moribund institution is evident in each part of his
description;[8] dull predictability and rigid conformity were
its key-notes, and he comments laconically that the only
'stimulating element in the teaching consisted of a few well-
used canes which hung on the green iron chimney-piece of
the single schoolroom'.

Nor did the fifteen-year-old Lewis enjoy his stay at
Malvern College, Worcestershire, as he explained in a letter
to Arthur Greeves in July 1914. In particular he objected to
the almost total lack of appreciation of books or music,[9] but
at least it taught him to view more favourably the life back

home in Belfast. He found the daily – to him endless – round of cricket and other sports dull and uninspiring, and he deliberately retreated from his companions whom he saw as lacking in brains and in refinement. In the same letter though, he does refer to the excellence of the school library which was evidently well-stocked, and he adds that he had found an author 'exactly after my own heart', W. B. Yeats, the Irish poet and literary figure. Mercifully the summer term of 1914 was to be his last at Malvern. Compulsory games he loathed, nor did he take kindly to what his brother calls in his 'Memoir to the Lewis Letters'[10], the 'standardizing Public School system'. Temperamentally, and certainly intellectually, he was utterly unsuited to life at Malvern and it was to his undisguised relief and for his profit that he came under the influence of William T. Kirkpatrick (1848–1921) at Great Bookham, Surrey.

Life now, and for the next two and a half years from September 1914, was congenial and mentally invigorating. A not untypical day[11] would start with breakfast at 8.00am, followed by a walk until about 9.15am, after which the morning was occupied with work, apart from a short break from 11–11.15am. Before the break, what he calls 'that glorious Iliad' would have been the subject, and then Latin until luncheon. The hours between 1 pm and 5.00 pm were usually free, but he worked for two hours until dinner at about 7.30pm. Reading a course in English literature frequently occupied the hours after dinner. For modern adolescents, this sort of timetable would be daunting, but not for Lewis, to whom it was the sort of life he would himself have chosen. The breadth and extent of his reading at this stage was quite staggering for a person of his age, and his mind, not surprisingly, developed brilliantly. Kirkpatrick described him as an 'exceptional student', high praise indeed. It was no surprise, therefore, when in 1916 he was elected to a scholarship at University College, Oxford. Writing to his father in December 1916,[12] he recorded in enthusiastic terms his first impressions of the city with the dreaming spires, declaring that it surpassed his wildest dreams. Lewis became an undergraduate in 1917, and in a letter post-marked 28th April[13] he gave an account of the effects of war on life at Oxford, a particularly notable feature being the small numbers at the colleges. At University College there were only six men, four of whom were 'freshmen', though others were to join them later. He was surprised to find his tutor doubling as the college Bursar, and also that no real reading had been recommended to him.

Lewis found another of the undergraduates, L. F. A. Edgell, uncongenial, partly because his tastes were not those shared by himself and Greeves, but primarily because Edgell was interested in mechanics.[14] He appears to have made few real friends at first – possibly none – but in general he found Oxford an 'absolutely ripping' place, and intellectually life was pleasant, with long talks about religion, literature, and 'everything else' featuring prominently in his daily routine. Other undergraduate customs were observed too, including getting drunk at a party to celebrate the 'Firsts' achieved by two University College men in 1917.

The First World War, however, was destined to interfere with his academic studies, and after military training in Devon which aroused in him neither great enthusiasm nor violent opposition, he spent his nineteenth birthday in France, experiencing the appalling conditions which have been graphically evoked by many poets, but by none more hauntingly than Wilfred Owen:

> Bent double, like old beggars under sacks,
> Knock-kneed, coughing like hags, we cursed through sludge,
> Till on the haunting flares we turned our backs
> And towards our distant rest began to trudge.
> Men marched asleep. Many had lost their boots
> But limped on, blood-shod. All went lame; all blind;
> Drunk with fatigue; deaf even to the hoots
> Of tired, outstripped Five-Nines that dropped behind.
>
> Gas! Gas! Quick, boys!—An ecstacy of fumbling,
> Fitting the clumsy helmets just in time;
> But someone still was yelling out and stumbling
> And flound'ring like a man in fire or lime ...
> Dim, through the misty panes and thick green light,
> As under a green sea, I saw him drowning.[15]

It was a war of appalling suffering and carnage; Britain and the Allies alone lost over five million men killed and almost thirteen million men wounded. At the Battle of the Somme, for example, on 1st July 1916, fifteen British soldiers were killed and twenty-five wounded each minute for twenty-four hours. It was for such as them that Wilfred Owen wrote his 'Anthem for Doomed Youth', those young men who 'died as cattle', victims of the 'stuttering rifles' rapid rattle'.[16]

Lewis's letters do not concentrate on the physical deprivations and agonies which inevitably accompany fighting and war. Rather frequently they refer to the reading he has done or the books he requires. On 4th January 1918, he asks his father to procure a cheap edition of the life of the novelist George Eliot, because he was at that time reading *Mill on the Floss*.[17] A similar note is struck in a letter to Arthur Greeves – he tells him that he has just finished *Adam Bede*, is reading Balzac's *Old Goriot*, and wants works by Boswell, Milton, and another novel by George Eliot.[18] There is something fascinating about a man who in the midst of war is concerned with his literary reading; perhaps he just realised that the latter was more enduring than the war.

He was, however, wounded by the explosion of an unstrategically placed English bomb during the Battle of Arras on 15th April 1918, and by 25th May he was in Endsleigh Hospital, London. His war was over. Discharge from the Army followed, and he was able to return to his studies at University College in 1919.

Few can emulate the sort of brilliant academic success he achieved: a 'First' in classical 'Mods' in 1920, a 'First' in classical 'Greats' in 1922, followed by yet another 'First' in honours English in 1923. To this impressive list can be added the Chancellor's English Prize in 1921. These successes, however, did not automatically ensure a fellowship for him and he accepted a temporary tutorship in Philosophy at University College. On 20th May 1925, aged 26, he was elected to an official fellowship in English Language and Literature at Magdalen College, Oxford, where he remained until he migrated to Magdalene College, Cambridge, in 1954.

Looking back over Lewis's early life, it is perfectly apparent that he was an imaginative, gifted, often quite lonely, and precocious child. He had very definite ideas about his own aptitudes and about life, so that it is not surprising that with his intellectual maturity he should have found boarding-school routine tiresome, restricting and difficult to endure. He preferred reading to compulsory games, and desperately needed the intellectual stimulation he ultimately found at Great Bookham. Emotionally too he required a secure base at a crucial period in his life, not least because his relationship with his father was so fraught and unsatisfactory. That he would enter the academic world was always likely; few people have been better suited for such a career. Reading was always a sheer delight to him: 'Talking about finishing books, I have at last come to the end of the Faerie Queene: and though I say "at last", I almost wish he had lived to write six books more as he hoped to do – so much have I enjoyed it.'[19] In another letter to Greeves he asks, 'What is nicer than to get a book – doubtful both about reading matter and edition, and then to find both are to topping.' Such genuine enthusiasm for books is rare even amongst gifted students.

The extracts quoted above are typical of the comments Lewis frequently makes in his letters to Greeves. Already, too, his conservative literary tendencies, so marked in later life, are firmly fixed.[20]

It must have been a highly rewarding experience for Kirkpatrick to teach a talented, industrious, discriminating, and mature student such as the seventeen-year-old Lewis, whose potential was immense.[21]

Tutor, Lecturer, and Scholar

Lewis's election to a fellowship at Magdalen was a considerable relief to him and, in a letter dated 26th May 1925, he expressed genuine gratitude to his father for generous support extended over a period of six years.

'You have waited, not only without complaint but full of encouragement, while chance after chance slipped away and when the goal receded farthest from sight. Thank you again and again.'[22]

His salary was to start at £500 a year with additional provision for rooms, pension, and dining. Initially the election was for five years only, but this might be – and, in fact, was – extended by his being re-elected. He was formally installed at Magdalen in August 1925, at a curious ceremony enacted before the whole college, at which the President of the college addressed the new Fellow in Latin for five minutes. The final part of the formalities seemed to him even more odd and stilted, because it consisted of each member of the college addressing him with the words, 'I wish you joy'.[23] After completing other less exalted tasks, like getting furniture and fittings for three large rooms in college, he settled down to prepare his lectures, a task requiring concentrated and real effort, so much so that his first Christmas holiday at home after his election was limited to a single week. All this arduous preparation, however, was rewarded.[24] His lecture-room was so over-crowded that another bigger room had to be found across the road, with the result that traffic in the High Street was held up while Lewis and the undergraduates surged across. It was a notable beginning, and the over-crowding at his lectures was to be a recurring Oxford phenomenon for many years.

Lewis was now firmly launched on his life-long career. That he was busy is obvious from the various glimpses he gives in his letters to Arthur Greeves. In one of them he says that it was only with the greatest difficulty that he was ever free to visit Oxford's shops.[25]

Much has been written about Lewis the tutor and lecturer, some of it accurate and realistic, some of it apocryphal and downright misleading; also, with something as subjective as teaching and tutoring, it is only to be expected that opinion about him should vary enormously. John Betjeman recalled his time under Lewis with no particular enthusiasm or enjoyment, and there is an interesting little entry in Lewis's journal for 27th May 1926 which shows that he was not particularly enamoured with the future famous poet either.[26] John Lawlor in his article, 'The Tutor and Scholar'[27], recalls vividly three aspects of Lewis's approach to his rôle as tutor. First there was his determined impersonality in his dealings with all except his closest friends. Then there was his remarkable mind, which was frequently bored with pupils of limited ability. When this happened the outcome was embarrassing for both pupil and tutor, and occasionally even the ablest of his pupils were reduced either to silence, or worse, to bumbling incoherence. Thirdly, there was Lewis's conservatism, best illustrated by his retort that for someone to ask for a tutor's help in reading literature by a contemporary figure was like asking for 'a nurse's assistance' to blow his own nose. Faced by this sort of reaction, it is not surprising, perhaps, that some students quailed before him, and this sort of comment led to the belief that Lewis hated the job of tutoring students, which was far from being the case. In later life certainly – especially after he migrated to Cambridge – it is true that he was glad to be relieved of the daily grind of seeing pupils and marking their work, but it would be unfair to project this back to his *whole* time at Oxford.

To George Bailey he was an 'interesting', 'colourful' and 'lively' tutor, but 'not a good teacher', the reasons suggested being that he did not have the gift for inspiring his students to enthusiasm: 'He lacked even the active interest in developing their capacities. He took his students as they came and took care only to make sure that they met the basic requirements to pass schools. Either he was not a very good judge of character or his lack of interest in his students prevented him from assessing them accurately.'[28] According to Bailey, however, it was a completely different matter in the lecture room:

'It was at the rostrum that he gave everything and took nothing – except the satisfaction of knowing that he was doing what he chose to do and doing it superbly. For it is here, I am convinced, that Lewis, the scholar, found his best fulfilment as a human being among his fellow men.'

Professor J. A. W. Bennett (Lewis's successor at Cambridge) agrees about his abilities as a teacher: 'Fine scholar though he was, he was an even better teacher.'[29] To Nevill Coghill, he was 'easily the greatest teacher of our time in his chosen fields'.[30] For a later view of Lewis I turned to Richard Thorpe, author-schoolmaster, a colleague of mine in the English department at Charterhouse. He was a student at Selwyn College, Cambridge from October 1962 – June 1965. He was advised by his supervisor, James Winny, to attend the lectures given by Lewis in Mill Lane, on the period 1300–1500. In an interview I had with Mr Thorpe he told me that although Lewis was scheduled to lecture at noon, he never actually started until ten minutes past the hour. His lectures were packed out with students, not all of them reading English. The only comparable 'star' on the arts side was Noel Annan, Provost, at the time, of King's College. Lewis spoke for something like 30–35 minutes without notes, then asked for questions, and this generally sparked off stimulating discussion. On one occasion Lewis was asked what the medievalists would like best if they returned to the present world. Would it be penicillin, space travel, or what? To this he replied that it 'would be the card-index system' used in libraries, because their love of hierarchy would endear this particular orderly system to them. According to Thorpe, Lewis talked rather than lectured in the formal sense implied by the word, carrying his vast learning easily and unobtrusively; he was richly anecdotal and down-to-earth. The only paper he had in front of him was a copy of the text being studied on that particular day. He frequently wrote on the blackboard. I asked about Lewis's reputed impersonality with students and was told that he was known amongst the Cambridge students for his friendliness and approachability; a mellower version of the Oxford Lewis!

Lectures, tutorials, faculty meetings, public lectures, marking examination papers, dining in college, companionship with his brother – not always appreciated by the other dons at Magdalen – writing his books, corresponding with people from all over the world, all gave Lewis's life a form, a discipline and a routine; seemingly a rather rigid and unexciting one to external observers. To these activities must be added his link with two societies, 'The Martlets' and 'The Inklings'. Both of these have been described at

length by Walter Hooper[31] and Humphrey Carpenter[32], so
that they need be referred to only briefly here.

The Martlets was a literary club at University College
which, he told his father in a letter dated 7th February 1919,
was limited to 'twelve undergraduate members'. In the same
letter he claimed (erroneously) that it had been in existence
for 'over three hundred years'. Each member took his turn to
host the session, and at each meeting a paper was read.
Lewis became secretary on 31st January 1919, upon enrolling
as a member. His first paper, on William Morris, was read by
a fellow student while Lewis took the minutes (on 12th
March 1919). His last, delivered on 14th November 1940, was
on 'The Kappa element in Romance', which subsequently
appeared in a considerably revised form as 'On Stories' in
Essays Presented to Charles Williams (Oxford 1947). After each
paper vigorous discussion followed, and perhaps some
abuse too. Other papers he presented before the gathered
Martlets included 'The poetry of Edmund Spenser', 'Boswell', 'The personal heresy in politics' and 'Is Literature
Art?'. Such occasions compelled him to clarify his ideas in
his own mind before submitting them to the eagle-eyed
scrutiny of his fellow undergraduates, and subsequently
defending them. More glamorous was 'The Inklings'. This
group met on Tuesday at lunch-time in the The Eagle and
Child public house – usually referred to as "The Bird and
Baby" because of its signboard depicting the Ganymede/
Jupiter story. On Thursday evenings members came to
Lewis's college rooms, to drink tea and beer and to read
excerpts from the books they were writing. According to
Carpenter, the group owed its existence to Lewis's inspira-
tion. Other members included J.R.R. Tolkien, Owen
Barfield, David Cecil, Nevill Coghill, Hugo Dyson, J.A.W.
Bennett, Christopher Tolkien, Gervase Mathew, and Lewis's
own brother, W. H. (Warnie) Lewis. The jovial, scholarly,
masculine atmosphere has been described in great detail by
Carpenter, so that there is no need to repeat the facts. These
meetings, however, were a fixed and important part of
Lewis's life and accorded well with his temperament and
natural inclinations: his liking for reading, argument, and
the company of those of kindred mind and spirit. Not all the

meetings, of course, were sparkling, and, as with any series, some were lethargic and desultory ones, but they were valuable. The society lasted until 1949, the final curtain being described thus by Carpenter:

> The end came almost imperceptibly, and for no apparent reason. The last Thursday Inklings to be recorded in Warnie Lewis's diary was on 20 October 1949, when there was a 'ham supper' in his brother's rooms. The next Thursday, 'No one turned up after dinner, which was just as well, as J. has a bad cold and wanted to go to bed early.' And the week after that: 'No Inklings tonight, so dined at home.' So vanished the Thursday Inklings. 'The best of them', said John Wain, 'were as good as anything I shall live to see.'[33]

By the nineteen-forties Lewis's reputation and prestige was immense, but the high standing he enjoyed as a scholar did not ensure for him what he so richly deserved: a professorial chair at Oxford. To an objective observer this was a truly amazing situation, though it is not difficult to suggest reasons *why* he was not suitably rewarded. In the first instance his world-wide fame as an apologist worked adversely against him as a scholar. An ambivalence was felt to exist between his Christian books, such as *The Screwtape Letters*, and his scholarly and academic works, though it is hard to say whether this was created, manufactured or imagined. Another factor, undoubtedly, was envy; human kind resents success in other people, and the plaudits Lewis received clearly annoyed some of his fellow dons at Magdalen, and in Oxford in general. Sheldon Vanauken relates a not untypical reaction to Lewis manifested when he was nominated for the Professorship of Poetry in 1951:

> Thad, who was walking along the High Street behind two dons, heard one of them remark: 'Shall we go and cast our votes against C. S. Lewis?' Not, that is, *for* the other chap.[34]

In the event, Cecil Day-Lewis was elected to the chair, the third nominee, Edmund Blunden, opting to drop out in order to deny Lewis the honour. Later, changes were made in the English syllabus which hived off medieval and

Renaissance studies from the solid core of 'modern literature'. Disheartened by this – in his view retrograde –
development in the English faculty Lewis felt free to accept
the chair of Medieval and Renaissance English at Cambridge. He wrote to an American correspondent on 1st
November 1954 about his new appointment:

> Did I tell you I've been made a professor at Cambridge? I take
> up my duties on Jan. 1st at Magdalene College, Cambridge
> (Eng.). Note the difference in spelling. It means rather less work
> for rather more pay. And I think I shall like Magdalene better
> than Magdalen. It's a tiny college (a perfect cameo architectural-
> ly) and they're all so old fashioned, and pious, and gentle and
> conservative – unlike this leftist, atheist, cynical, hard-boiled,
> huge Magdalen.[35]

The last sentence reflects clearly his unfavourable view of
the post-war changes at Oxford, which encouraged one of
Oxford's most famous sons to turn to 'the other place'. His
time at Cambridge was extremely happy and friendly, and
mercifully he was released from the grind of routine tutorials and other irksome duties. Dr G. M. Trevelyan revealed
– on the night of Lewis's inaugural lecture, *De Descriptione
Temporum*[36] – that his election to the specially created chair
had received 'complete unanimity of votes on the part of the
committee',[37] surely an unusual situation. If he had been a
prophet without honour in his own country, he was duly
accorded that honour at Cambridge, and utterly deserved it
too. Happy and contented, these were years of 'mellow'
enjoyment. Clearly the death in 1960 of his wife, Joy,[38]
caused him pain and suffering, notwithstanding that at the
time of their marriage in 1957, he had known that, he
'married (knowingly) a very sick, save by a near miracle, a
dying woman'.[39] These feelings of grief and loss he poured
out in a small book entitled *A Grief Observed*. With Joy gone,
Lewis turned increasingly to his work for consolation and
solace. Henceforth his life was dominated by increasing
illness and disability. He struggled on at Cambridge until
the middle of June 1963. Patient in the face of considerable
suffering and discomfort, he accepted the inevitable end
calmly and stoically:

With peace and consolation hath dismissed,
And calm of mind, all passion spent.[40]

His death, occurring on the same day as that of President
Kennedy, was little noticed, but later his memory received
its full and due recognition.

CHAPTER THREE

Visionary and Allegorist

John Bunyan's *Pilgrim's Progress* (Part One 1678, Part Two 1684) is one of the greatest creative works of the seventeenth-century. It is all the more significant because it was published in an otherwise barren period in the history of English fiction: 'If in some ways Bunyan's best work represents a culmination of certain kinds of seventeenth-century Puritan writing, in others it looks forward to the development of the English novel. His interest in spiritual autobiography and cautionary allegory stems from a long Puritan tradition which in turn had roots in medieval religious thought and expression; his method of translating his theological ideas into vivid, realistic, contemporary terms, reflecting with immediacy the daily life and conversation of the ordinary people of England, shows the technique of the embryo novelist.'[1]

Bunyan views man's life as a journey, with Christian travelling from the City of Destruction to the glory and resplendent majesty of Heaven, the entrance to which is barred by a river:

This River has been a Terror to may, yea the thoughts of it also have often frighted me. But now methinks I stand easie, my Foot is fixed upon that, upon which the Feet of the Priests that bare the Ark of the Covenant stood while *Israel* went over this *Jordan*. The Waters indeed are to the Palate bitter, and to the Stomack cold; yet the thoughts of what I am going to, and of the Conduct that waits for me on the other side, doth lie as a glowing Coal at my Heart.

I see my self now at the *end* of my Journey, my *toilsom* Days are ended. I am going now to see *that* Head that was Crowned with Thorns, and *that* Face that was spit upon, for me.

Thus the closing scenes of the *Pilgrim's Progress* are notable for their assurance and sublime confidence:

> But glorious it was, to see how the open Region was filled with Horses and Chariots, with Trumpeters and Pipers, with Singers, and Players on stringed Instruments, to welcome the Pilgrims as they went up and followed one another in at the beautiful Gate of the City.[2]

Bunyan's vision has become a permanent part of Britain's literary and religious heritage, with a vigorously expressed message that has transcended each age. The fact that it has been translated into nearly a hundred and fifty languages is eloquent testimony to its ability to reach and to influence the thinking of people of different cultures, temperaments and nationalities. The formally uneducated Bunyan was altogether different from the man who just over two hundred and fifty years later gave the world another vision and allegory. Lewis had published poetry – *Spirits in Bondage* (1919) and *Dymer* (1926) – but *The Pilgrim's Regress*, published in 1933, was his first major prose work. When it appeared Tolkien is reputed to have said that 'Lewis would regress', adding: 'He would not re-enter Christianity by a new door, but by the old one: at least in the sense that in taking it up again he would also take up again, or re-awaken, the old prejudices so sedulously planted in childhood and boyhood. He would become again a Northern Ireland protestant.'[3] I assume however that the 'Regress' of the title (which is taken up at the head of Book 10 and so is not to be interpreted ironically) refers to the *movement* of the book. That is, John starts quite near the Landlord's castle, and mother Kirk would have taken him there directly. But he sets off on his own, and thus takes an age to reach Christian initiation (baptism and the gift of the Holy Spirit). So far this has seemed like progress, but now he must retrace his steps (regress) – though the return journey, followed swiftly by crossing the Brook, is very different from his earlier wanderings.

If we are to understand *The Pilgrim's Regress* we must refer to Lewis's spiritual experience up to the year 1933, an aspect not alluded to in chapter 2 of this work. He has left a full account of his childhood, education, and university life in *Surprised by Joy*, first published in 1955. The first thirteen chapters of this work, however, hardly refer to religious matters, although, as the reviewer of the Hooper and Green biography in the *Times Literary Supplement*[4] wryly suggested, Lewis's Ulster background and evangelical antecedents meant that eventually religion would catch up with him, as it did in a most striking way.

The main lines of the story are preserved in chapters 14 ('Checkmate') and 15 ('The Beginning') of *Surprised by Joy*. Having finished classical 'Greats' in the summer of 1922 he entered for the English School, and there in George Gordon's discussion class he encountered Nevill Coghill. Hitherto an atheist, Lewis was shocked to discover that Coghill, whom he considered to be 'the most intelligent and best informed man in the class', was also 'a Christian and a thoroughgoing supernaturalist'. But there were many other influences too, or patterns in the overall mosaic. One such was Owen Barfield, whom Lewis referred to as his 'Second Friend', and who is differentiated from his 'First Friend' in this way: The First is the *alter ego*, the man who first reveals to you that you are not alone in the world by turning out (beyond hope) to share all your secret delights. There is nothing to overcome in making him your friend; he and you join like rain-drops on a window. But the second Friend is the man who disagrees with you about everthing. He is not so much the *alter ego* as the anti-self.'[5] They did, it was true, share many mutual interests, but they approached them from different viewpoints. Barfield was instrumental, firstly in destroying what Lewis calls his 'chronological snobbery', defined as the uncritical acceptance of 'the intellectual climate common to our own age and the assumption that whatever has gone out of date is on that account discredited'[6] and secondly, in demonstrating that the view of the 'realists' was inconsistent.[7]

There were literary pressures too. He found that George MacDonald was a good writer in spite of his Christianity, while Chesterton appeared to him to possess far more sense than all the moderns' put together'. On the other hand, some writers, including Shaw, Gibbon and Voltaire, came to be a little insubstantial in his estimation; they also lacked the 'roughness and density of life'. Perhaps most influential of all was the poetry of George Herbert, who seemed to Lewis to excel all the authors he had ever read in being able to convey and portray 'the very quality of life as it's lived from moment to moment'.

All that remained was to inquire a little more closely 'whether the Christians were, after all, wrong'. He did not take this apparently natural step, but the chase was on; he was being pursued by the 'Hound of Heaven' who followed him with 'unhurrying chase ... and unperturbed pace'.[8] Using the analogy of a game of chess, Lewis then relates how his Adversary's next move was intellectual. He read *Space, Time and Deity*, in which Alexander expounds his theory of 'Enjoyment' and 'Contemplation'. He understood these terms in the following way: 'When you see a table you enjoy the act of seeing and contemplate the table. Later if you took up Optics and thought about Seeing itself, you would be contemplating the seeing and enjoying the thought. In bereavement you contemplate the beloved and the beloved's death and, in Alexander's sense, enjoy the loneliness and the grief, but a psychologist, if he were considering you as a case of melancholia, would be contemplating your grief and enjoying psychology.'[9] This convinced Lewis that his life's search for Joy had been a 'futile attempt to contemplate the enjoyed'. The next step was the realisation that he had been utterly wrong in supposing that he had actually desired Joy itself; the corollary was the understanding that 'all the value lay in that of which Joy was the desiring'. There came this piercing insight:

I saw that Joy, as I now understood it, would fit in. We mortals, seen as the sciences see us and as we commonly see one another, are mere "appearances". But appearances of the Absolute. In so far as we really are at all (which isn't saying much) we have, so to speak, a root in the Absolute, which is the utter reality. And that is why we experience Joy: we yearn, rightly, for that unity which we can never reach except by ceasing to be the separate phenomenal beings called "we". Joy was not a deception.[10]

He still felt, however, that there was no possibility of entering into personal relations with the 'Absolute' (or 'Him', or 'Spirit'). Chesterton's *Everlasting Man* convinced him that Christianity itself was eminently sensible, while it gradually dawned upon him that Idealism cannot be lived out. To go on thinking of the 'Spirit' as oblivious of, or indeed passive to, personal approaches, was clearly untenable. What was needed now was nothing less than a total and complete surrender, or, to use a different metaphor, 'the absolute leap in the dark'. That Lewis continued 'to kick against the pricks' is evidenced by his remark, years later, to Sheldon Vanauken,[11] that he hoped very strongly that Christianity was not true. The demand for 'all' had to be answered affirmatively, for God was closing in on him, and eventually, in the Trinity Term of 1929, he gave in, admitting that 'God was God'. He knelt and prayed, in his now famous words, 'the most dejected and reluctant convert in all England'.[12] With typical eloquence he portrays himself as a 'kicking, struggling, resentful' convert, eagerly looking everywhere for the chance to escape the divine – and by now inexorable – clutches.

Lewis had now journeyed from atheism to theism, for the God to whom he had surrendered was 'sheerly non-human'. As yet he was not concerned about the Incarnation nor about the future life. The final transition to Christianity could not be – and was not – long delayed. It occurred, in fact, as Lewis was being driven to Whipsnade Zoo one sunny morning. At the outset of his journey he had no belief in Jesus Christ as the Son of God but by the time he reached the zoo he did have just that belief.[13] Lewis's somewhat curious statement does not indicate how the change was effected, and students of Lewis's life must accept the version as it stands, always remembering how inscrutable are the ways of the Holy Spirit in dealing with a man's soul. Predictably it was to Arthur Greeves he wrote, explaining that he had just 'passed from believing in God to definitely

believing in Christ—in Christianity'.[14] In the same letter
Lewis indicates that Tolkien and Dyson had also had a
good deal to do with his conversion to full-blooded
Christianity;[15] and in another letter to Greeves he gives a
full and personal account of what occurred on the night of
19th September 1931:

> Now what Dyson and Tolkien showed me was this: that if I
> met the idea of sacrifice in a Pagan story I didn't mind it at all:
> again, that if I met the idea of a god sacrificing himself to himself
> (cf. the quotation opposite the title page of *Dymer*) I liked it very
> much and was mysteriously moved by it: again, that the idea of
> the dying and reviving God (Balder, Adonis, Bacchus) similarly
> moved me provided I met it anywhere *except* in the Gospels.
> The reason was that in Pagan stories I was prepared to feel the
> myth as profound and suggestive of meanings beyond my grasp
> even tho' I could not say in cold prose 'what it meant'.
>   Now the story of Christ is simply a true myth: a myth working
> on us in the same way as the others, but with this tremendous
> difference that *it really happened*: and one must be content to
> accept it in the same way, remembering that it is God's myth
> where the others are men's myths: i.e. the Pagan stories are God
> expressing Himself through the minds of poets, using such
> images as He found there, while Christianity is God expressing
> Himself through what we call 'real things'. Therefore it is *true*,
> not in the sense of being a 'description' of God (that no finite
> mind could take in) but in the sense of being the way in which
> God chooses to (or can) appear to our faculties. The 'doctrines'
> we get *out of* the true myth are of course *less* true: they are
> translations into our *concepts* and *ideas* of that wh. God has
> already expressed in a language more adequate, namely the
> actual incarnation, crucifixion, and resurrection. Does this
> amount to a belief in Christianity? At any rate I am now certain
> (a) That this Christian story is to be approached, in a sense, as I
> approach the other myths. (b) That it is the most important and
> full of meaning. I am also *nearly* certain that it really happened.[16]

Thus there are two crucial dates to be borne in mind when
thinking of Lewis's progress towards belief in Christianity,
one in 1929, the other in 1931. It is to a date midway between
these two that we can trace the genesis of *The Pilgrim's
Regress*, because on 29th April 1930 his letter to Greeves

included four stanzas which later, and in a considerably
revised form, appeared in *The Pilgrim's Regress*, in Book 10
chapter 7 (headed 'Luxuria'), as the verses composed by
John while attempting to shut out the insidious temptations
of the Witch:

> When Lilith means to draw me
> Within her secret bower,
> She does not overawe me
> With beauty's pomp and power,
> Nor, with angelic grace
> Of courtesy, and the pace
> Of gliding ships, comes veiled at evening hour.
>
> Eager, unmasked, she lingers
> Heart-sick and hunger sore;
> With hot, dry, jewelled fingers
> Stretched out, beside her door,
> Offering with gnawing haste
> Her cup, whereof who taste,
> (She promises no better) thirst far more.
>
> What moves me, then, to drink it?
> – Her spells, which all around
> So change the land, we think it
> A great waste where a sound
> Of wind like tales twice told
> Blusters, and cloud is rolled
> Always above yet no rain falls to ground
>
> Across drab iteration
> Of bare hills, line on line,
> The long road's sinuation
> Leads on. The witch's wine,
> Though promising nothing, seems
> In that land of no streams,
> To promise best – the unrelished anodyne.[17]

Later, on 28th August 1930, writing to Greeves, he refers in
general terms to some religious lyrics which he had written
during the preceding year, adding that he had taken great
pains[18] in order to get the best possible version of them. In
the same letter he says that if the book reached an audience

of only one it had as much justification as if it reached an audience of thousands. He then adds something which shows to what an extent he needed, indeed was compelled to write; for to Lewis writing was, like reading, an act as vital as breathing itself: 'I am sure that some are born to write as trees are born to bear leaves: for these, writing is a necessary mode of their own development. If the impulse to write survives the hope of success, then one is among these.'[19] So not only did he have an inherent desire to write and to communicate, but writing was for him both a part of his development, and, in some instances, a means of purging, as can be seen in *A Grief Observed*. That writing came easily to him made the whole process less laborious than for many people.

Two years, however, elapsed before the book was actually written during a fortnight's holiday in Ireland in August 1932, when, according to Lewis, it 'spurted out'[20] The phrase evokes Bunyan's statement, 'For having now my Method by the end;/Still as I pull'd, it came.' Bunyan gives no additional detail about the process we know of as 'inspiration'. It is, though, perfectly reasonable to conjecture why it occurred at that precise moment. Lewis's guess was 'that the scheme of the journey with adventures suddenly re-united two things in Bunyan's mind which had hitherto lain far apart. One of these was his life-long preoccupation with the life of the Spirit, the other was something Bunyan had left behind long ago: his delight in old wives' tales and such last remnants of chivalric romance as he had found in chap-books. The one fitted the other like a glove. Now, as never before, the whole man was engaged.'[21] In the case of Bunyan, such an ecstatic experience probably implied an absence of objective judgement, but it is unlikely that the same could be said of the Magdalen don.

Prior to being shown to Owen Barfield, the manuscript was apparently submitted to Arthur Greeves for his comments and criticism, because on 4th December 1932 Lewis says that whereas Greeves wanted a more correct and classical, indeed 'elaborate' manner,[22] Lewis aimed at being 'idiomatic and racy'. Nevertheless he took Greeves's detailed criticisms seriously and in a further letter, thirteen days later, dealt carefully with them.

I. *Quotations.* I hadn't realised that they were so numerous as you apparently found them. Mr Sensible, as you rightly saw, is in a separate position: the shower of quotations is part of the character and it wd. be a waste of time to translate them, since the dialogue (I hope) makes it clear that his quotations were always silly and he always missed the point of the authors he quoted. The other ones may be too numerous, and perhaps can be reduced & translated. But not beyond a certain point: for one of the contentions of the book is that the decay of our old classical learning is a contributory cause of atheism (see the chapter on Ignorantia). The quotations at the beginnings of the Books are of course never looked at at all by most readers, so I don't think they matter much.

2. *Simplicity.* I expect your dissatisfaction on this score points to some real, perhaps v. deep seated, fault: but I am sure it cannot be remedied – least of all in a book of controversy. Also there may be some real difference of conception between you and me. You remember we discussed last summer how much more sympathy you had than I with the Puritan simplicity. I doubt if I interpret Our Lord's words quite in the same way as you. I think they mean that the *spirit* of man must become humble and trustful like a child and, like a child, *simple in motive*, i.e. disinterested, not scheming and 'on the look out'. I don't think He meant that adult Christians must *think* like children: still less that the processes of thought by wh. people *become* Christians must be childish processes. At any rate the *intellectual* side of my conversion was *not* simple and I can describe only what I know. Of course it is only too likely that much of the thought in P.R. offends against simplicity simply by being confused or clumsy! And where so, I wd. gladly emend it if I knew how.[23]

By Christmas 1932 the manuscript had been revised and Lewis informed Greeves that the work would appear by the end of May 1933, as indeed it did, bearing the following title: *The Pilgrim's Regress: An Allegorical Apology for Christianity, Reason and Romanticism.* The proof copy had contained the phrase 'or Pseudo-Bunyan's Periplus' inserted between the words 'Regress' and 'An'. Lewis had tried to resist the shortening of the title but had been defeated. That the publication had been anything but smooth is clear in his letter to Greeves, because on 25th March 1933 he refers to his

successful attempt to resist the wishes of the publishers who
wanted to bring out an illustrated edition.

In financial terms *The Pilgrim's Regress* was a failure, and
fewer than 700 of the 1,000 copies printed were sold. In 1935
the Roman Catholic publishers, Sheed and Ward, bought
the book from Dent. Lewis objected to a 'Papist' publisher
bringing out one of his religious books, but he gave in
because Sheed and Ward thought they could sell it whereas
Dent patently could not. There was yet one more conten-
tious issue, for a letter to Greeves in December 1935 carried
this aggrieved paragraph:

> Sheed, without any authority from me, has put a blurb on the
> inside of the jacket which says 'This story begins in Puritania
> (Mr Lewis was brought up in Ulster)' – thus implying that the
> book is an attack on my own country and my own religion. If
> you ever come across any one who might be interested, explain
> as loudly as you can that I was not consulted & that the blurb is a
> damnable lie told to try and make Dublin riff-raff buy the
> book.[24]

In ten books, *The Pilgrim's Regress* tells of the spiritual
adventures of a boy called John who lives in Puritania. It is a
beautiful country, but life there is constrained by rigid
prohibitions laid down by the 'Steward', who does so on the
authority of the 'Landlord', the owner of the whole country.

The time comes when John is forced to put on the ugliest
clothes he has ever seen in order to visit the Steward, who
turns out to be 'an old man with a red, round face, who was
very kind and full of jokes so that John quite got over his
fears'. But after a friendly chat about fishing and bicycles,
the Steward describes the Landlord as a 'very, very kind'
person who would nevertheless punish anybody who broke
the rules. 'He'd take you and shut you up for ever and ever
in a black hole full of snakes and scorpions as large as
lobsters – for ever and ever! And besides that, he is such a
kind, good man, so very, very kind, that I am sure you
would never *want* to displease him.'

In contrast to this experience of life, John has a vision of a
distant beautiful Island, which causes him to forget his fear

of the Landlord and the burdens and prohibitions of life in general. He develops an intense determination to seek out the island. One day, when his longing is almost unbearable, 'he thought he heard a voice saying, Come ... Among the hills of the western horizon, he thought that he saw a shining sea, and a faint shape of an Island, not much more than a cloud. It was nothing compared with what he had seen the first time; it was so much further away. But his mind was made up. That night he waited till his parents were asleep, and then, putting some few needments together, he stole out by the back door and set his face to the West to seek for the Island.'

Book Two tells how John left his home and met Mr Enlightenment, 'a big man with red hair and a red stubble on all his three chins, buttoned up very tight'. He invites John to travel westwards with him in his 'neat little trap' drawn by a 'fat little pony'. After an exchange of trivialities, Mr Enlightenment assures John, 'There is no Landlord! There is absolutely no such thing – I might even say no such *entity* – in existence. There has never has been and never will be.' He invites John into the 'magnificent' city of Claptrap, but John, although re-assured and profoundly relieved by what he has heard, refuses to enter the city. Next he encounters Mr Vertue coming up the hill towards him, and almost immediately they meet Media Halfways who invites John to visit her father who lives in the 'city of Thrill'. Attracted by Media he agrees, but Mr Vertue goes 'on his way stumping up the next hill without ever looking back'. After kissing each other and talking in 'slow voices, of sad and beautiful things', Media assures John: 'This is love ... this is the way to the real island', and Mr Halfways confirms her opinion by declaring that it is to be in 'one another's hearts'. The idyllic mood is shattered by the appearance of Gus Halfways, however, who greets the 'lovers' with a huge guffaw, after which they separate from each other instantly. The next morning Gus and John, seated on a machine renowned for its dynamic power, roar off across the country at speed to the north of the main road and find themselves in the city of Eschropolis where all the houses are constructed of steel.

Here, at the beginning of Book Three, John comes across The Clevers. 'The girls had short hair and flat breasts and flat buttocks so that they looked like boys: but the boys had pale, egg-shaped faces and slender waists and big hips so that they looked like girls – except for a few of them who had long hair and beards.' Soon, however, he annoys them. He is 'kicked in the back and belly, and tripped up so that he fell on his face, and hit again as he rose, and all the glass in the world seemed breaking around his head as he fled for his life from the laboratory'. As he does so, he hears the Clevers crying 'Puritanian! Bourgeois! Prurient'. Covered in filth and mud, he meets Mr Mammon, smoking a big cigar, who tells him that *he* owns Eschropolis. Proceeding westwards, he is arrested by armed men for attempting to leave the country belonging to the 'Spirit of the Age'. Put in chains and taken to a dirty prison hewn out of rocks, John discovers that his jailor is Sigismund Enlightenment, who has long since quarrelled with his Father. After some days in the prison, John is taken to be tried and punished by the giant 'Spirit of the Age'. He is saved, however, by the arrival of a woman wearing a 'cloak of blue' and seated on a 'great black stallion'. Her name is Reason and after she has plunged her sword into the giant's heart, 'the huge carcass settled down: and the Spirit of the Age became what he had seemed to be at first, a sprawling hummock of rock.' So ends Book Three.

Athough the prisoners are now free to escape, they choose to remain in the filth and darkness, offering as explanation: 'It is one more wish-fulfilment dream.' But John and Reason travel on together; he learns that her sisters are Philosophy and Theology. As they journey she points out the weaknesses of the Spirit of the Age and John realises, with concern, that Reason is apparently implying that the Landlord truly exists. After a tortuous journey, he returns alone to the main road, 'with his face towards the setting sun'.

In Book Five, John continues westward and again meets Vertue, who has been travelling 'scarcely ten miles a day'. As they journey forward together, John is startled to discover that the road he stands on runs up to the edge of a precipice. 'The chasm might be seven miles wide, and as for its length, it stretched southward on its left and northward on its right as far as he could see.' Vertue encourages John to cross the canyon, but he remains sceptical of his chance of success. While discussing, they are startled by an old woman, Mother Kirk, who tells them that their only chance of success is if *she* carries them down. Rejecting her offer of assistance, they retreat to the main road to discuss their plans, then travel northwards along the canyon. After walking a mile or so they come to Mr Sensible's house. After a chilly night and an encounter with an irascible Mr Sensible, Vertue and John continue their journey northward along the canyon. Mr Sensible's servant, Drodge, decides to come with them.

In Book Six they pursue a path up a bleak tableland, so bleak, in fact, that if they stopped, 'the sweat grew cold on them instantly'. Vertue's pace never alters or slackens, but John's feet grow sore and he begins to lag behind. Many miles further on, they take refuge in 'a little shanty' near the roadside, inhabited by three men, 'very thin and pale', called Mr Neo-Angular, Mr Neo-Classical, and Mr Humanist who explains: 'We are united by a common antagonism to a common enemy' ... You must understand that we are three brothers, the sons of Mr Enlightenment of the town of Claptrap.' After yet another unpleasant and uncomfortable night, Drudge and Vertue set out northwards, leaving John in conversation with Mr Humanist, but late that evening Vertue returns because there is no road over the gorge northward. This ends Book Six.

Drudge having remained behind, Vertue and John go towards the south. John confesses that his heart is about to break because he has lost, for the moment, the intensity of the sweet desire he had for the Island. Conscience can no longer guide John who gives up moral questions in despair. Eventually they confront Mr Broad who represents 'modern' Christianity. Bland but friendly, his attitude to John's request for advice on how to reach the island is typically evasive and unhelpful; every person, he says, has to find his own key to 'the mystery'. They next encounter Wisdom, sitting, like an old man, among his children. He advises them that, on the one hand, they have to avoid thinking, like the southern people, that the Island has a real identity and, on the other hand, they must also reject the views of the northern people who claim that 'the eastern and western things are merely illusions in your own minds.' From Wisdom's house the travellers must cross the impassable Valley of Wisdom, which is also be Valley of Humiliation.

The beginning of Book Eight finds Vertue and John continuing their journey, towered over by the cliffs, and John realises that they are, in fact, walking on a ledge midway down one side of the Grand Canyon. Once again, John feels disillusioned, indeed in his despair he is prepared to turn back altogether rather than attempt to climb the spur which now blocks the path. Deserted by Vertue, John is pushed and pulled to the top by a mysterious Man who later feeds him with bread, which, although its taste is flat and not altogether agreeable, sustains him for the journey.

During this stage of the journey, John has learned a number of fundamental lessons. One is that he must accept God's grace or die, although once having accepted God's grace, he must acknowledge God's existence. The second is that the Landlord may intend him for something utterly different from anything he has been taught to desire. Thirdly, all attempts at self-preservation must be abandoned entirely.

John eventually crawls in terror down the narrow ledge, only to find at the bottom of the canyon a pool which bars his way across, and thus prevents him from continuing his journey to the Island. Mother Kirk encourages him to plunge beneath the water to find the tunnel which (she assures him) lies within the cliff beneath the water. Stripped of his clothes, John is assailed by the wraiths of old Enlightenment, Media Halfways, old Halfways, young Halfways, Sigismund, Sensible, Broad, and the Humanists. Having survived what seemed likely to be a watery death, John and Vertue find themselves among a great company of other pilgrims. John has a vision of the Island and is presently allotted a Guide, who explains – to John's amazement – that the mountains which John can now see are both the Island, and also the very same mountains that he could see close at hand when he lived in Puritania. In fact the only way that John can reach the Island is to turn round and retrace his steps. However, the Guide consoles him with the assurance that the whole country will look very different 'on the return journey'. So Book Nine ends with John facing a Regress to the East.

The journey back, as described in Book Ten, is totally different. The house of Mr Sensible, has disappeared – as the Guide explains, Sensible is so shadowy that he is no longer visible to their renewed eyes. They pass Limbo, where Mr Wisdom (it now appears) has his home. They see Superbia, Ignorantia, and Luxuria, and after defeating the Northern Dragon, John reaches Puritania. At this point, the dream 'was full of light and noise ... they went on their way, singing and laughing like schoolboys.' Here in Puritania, John sees once more the brook which must be crossed by anybody who wishes to reach the mountains where the Landlord dwells. John's eyes fill with tears as he sees his parent's cottage, empty and ruined, and realises that they have already gone beyond the brook. The Guide reassures him that he himself will cross the brook shortly. Darkness has fallen before they cross, the voice of the Guide mingling in song with those of John and Vertue.

The main aspects of the allegory may be considered under five headings:

1. *Man's Essential Longing*

   The Island – represents the soul's acute yet delightful longing for an unknown object which is in fact God himself.

2. *Substitutes for/Denials of this Longing*

   The naked brown girl – represents lust as a substitute.

   Media Halfways and her father – advocate aesthetic experience as a substitute.

   Vertue – represents the moral imperative, grounded in pagan values, not attached to God nor fully understanding itself.

   The Clevers – are trendy, 'artistic' people who have had their inhibitions and rationality eroded by modern psychological teaching.

   Mr Enlightenment – represents nineteenth century rationalism, committed to explaining religion away.

Sigismund Enlightenment – represents Sigmund Freud, who is closely linked to the Spirit of the Age.

3. *'Mere' Christianity (Lewis's own phrase, though not in this book)*

   Mother Kirk – this name was chosen, according to Lewis because 'Christianity' seemed not to be a very convincing name. She warns the pilgrims that they cannot cross the canyon without her help and explains how the canyon came into existence. Their journey is all the longer because they decline to be carried down by her. Finally, she is the one who explains that without diving into the water they cannot reach the other side.

   The Guide – represents the Holy Spirit who leads them after their 'baptism'.

4. *Alternatives to 'Mere' Christianity*

   Mr Broad – stands for a Christianity deprived of the miraculous and the supernatural.

   Mr Wisdom – stands for the study of metaphysics which retains the desire of the soul but has no hope of ever attaining it.

   Three pale men – Mr Neo-Angular, Mr Neo-Classical and Mr Humanist – represent catholicism, classicism and humanism. They are all children of Mr Enlightenment, and they share a common hatred of the arts, the Spirit of the Age, and any form of compromise.

The straight road which carries the pilgrim past the City of Claptrap between the tableland of the High Anglicans, on the one hand, and the marshes of the Theosophists, on the other, represents traditional Christianity.[30]

Inevitably, much in Lewis's allegory is radically different from that of Bunyan – we may refer to his giants and to the Pilgrim's battle with the Northern Dragon. Yet for Bunyan and Lewis alike, the device of allegory makes it possible to say succinctly and powerfully what would normally require a full-length theological dissertation.

What are the positive qualities and achievements of *The Pilgrim's Regress*? In the first place, it makes perfectly explicit Lewis's understanding of *Sehnsucht* or Joy (that intense longing which draws a man towards God), by illustrating –

unlike the work of Bunyan – the motives for pursuing the pathway of traditional Christianity as they are present in the romantic imagination. The complex, often baffling, relationship between erotic and aesthetic experience is examined, and the relationship of these with religion, though Lewis's conclusions are radically different from those of both D. H. Lawrence and Freud. In short – his vision is thoroughly Christian. It is impossible to over-estimate the importance of Joy (graphically described by Lewis as the 'serious business of heaven') in his thinking and works. For him, it is no superficial emotion but the essential key to understanding man's very nature and also the nature of the creator. In *In Encounter with Light* he posed several questions that are higly relevant to this issue, the most serious being: 'If you are really the product of a materialistic universe, how is it that you don't feel at home there?'

The deepest thirst within man, as he says in *The Pilgrim's Regress*, 'is not adapted to the deepest nature of the world'. Indeed it is a desire to be 're-united with something in the universe from which we now feel cut off. ... no neurotic fancy, but the truest index of our real situation'. Alongside this is the awareness that our whole being, by its very nature, 'is one vast need; incomplete, preparatory, empty yet cluttered, crying out for Him who can untie things that are now knotted together and tie up things that are still dangling loose'.[31] Clearly linked with this idea of joy is the awareness that this desire cannot be satisfied with anything in this world: man is a solitary pilgrim:

There have been times when I think we do not desire heaven; but more often I find myself wondering whether in our heart of hearts we ever desired anything else. ... It is the secret signature of each soul, the incommunicable and unappeasable want, the thing we desired before we met our wives or made our friends or chose our work, and which we shall still desire on our deathbeds, when the mind no longer knows wife or friend or work. ... All our life an unattainable ecstasy has hovered just beyond the grasp of our consciousness. The day is coming when you will wake to find, beyond all hope, that you have attained it, or else, that it was within your reach and you have lost it forever.[32]

Joy then, as linked with the idea of man's religious quest in the world, challenges us to make a decision. The is quite explicit in John's encounter with Mr Broad (recounted in chapter 5). At first John and Mr Broad discuss Mr Sensible's character and conclude that his heart is in 'the right place'; later Mr Broad makes the trite comment that no person is 'perfect'. This, understandably, fails to satisfy John who needs precise directions on how to continue his quest for 'an island in the West'. What John really wants to know is whether the canyon has to be crossed, whether that definitive act is vitally and fundamentally necessary. Again, Mr Broad can offer nothing but soothing platitudes, including this one: 'Great truths need re-interpretation in every age.'[33]

The fact is that the canyon has to be crossed, and Mr Broad's response is utterly ineffective and totally evasive. Translated into New Testament terms, the gospel has to be faced up to, a decision has to be made, either negatively or positively. We must not avoid the realities which religious symbols only imperfectly represent: We must exercise responsibility, as Lewis himself had done. Lewis sees this pathway as avoiding the extremes of dogmatism (the rigid, compartmentalised system of the 'North') and emotionalism (the 'South', inhabited by the uncritical and the unthinking). Instead he envisages both the intellect and the feelings playing a balanced rôle in the relationship between God and man. It is a route in which reason is important, indeed vital. In fact, it is Reason which forces John to return to Mother Kirk. It is also a pathway which avoids rigid moralism; the observance of religious regulations is not a basic requirement, whereas genuine repentance is. Lewis objects to the cant, hypocrisy and artificiality which so frequently disfigure religious instruction. In chapter 1, for example, he abhors the 'sing-song' voice of the masked Steward when discussing the rôle and function of the Landlord; after their chat it is significant that the Steward 'took off the mask and had a nice sensible chat with John again'.[34] Christianity was not – nor was it intended to be – a mask with pseudo-observance of rules; it is meant to permeate the whole personality.

In *The Pilgrim's Regress* then, Lewis pursued two themes

in particular – his own conversion on the one hand, and, on the other, an attempt to unify all Christians of all denominations against contemporary religious and philosophical fashions. His prose is typically enchanting and lucid, and it can be argued that *The Pilgrim's Regress* is as remarkable and important as any of his other works.

Yet it has been curiously neglected – in the long and short term – both by the general public and by Lewis devotees. The reasons for this are many and varied. He refused to render into English the Greek and Latin quotations he included in the body of the book. His contention was that the 'decay of our old classical learning is a contributory cause of atheism'. To many this might well seem unnecessarily élitist. In addition, the route he followed was unfamiliar to the vast majority. He himself recognised that one of the book's chief faults was, in his own words, its 'needless obscurity', and in his 'Preface' to the third edition he tried to deal with the causes of this obscurity.[35] Another possible reason may be traced to the very fact that it was his first religious prose work: 'I didn't then know how to make things easy.' Also, *The Pilgrim's Regress* was published *before* he became a famous and well-known writer and broadcaster, and in all the acclaim that later attended such works as *The Screwtape Letters* and the *Narnia* chronicles, it tended to be neglected. A further complication arose, albeit inadvertently, as a result of the publicity blurb produced by the publishers Sheed and Ward. The statement they placed on the inside of the jacket, 'This story begins in Puritania (Mr Lewis was brought up in Ulster)', seemed to imply (and certainly Lewis felt this to be the implication) that the work was an attack on his own religion in general, and on Ireland in particular.

The Pilgrim's Regress is of special interest as the first account of Lewis's conversion; it thus has more immediacy than *Surprised by Joy*, which appeared in 1955. It also contains certain important emphases which occur frequently in his later work. He has no use for the people he contemptuously describes as the 'Clevers'. Later, in the first chapter of *The Voyage of the Dawn Treader* he talks about 'very up-to-date and advanced people' who were 'vegetarians, non-smokers and teetotallers and wore a special kind of underclothes'. Their houses contained only the minimum of furniture with 'very few clothes on the beds and the windows were always open'. In chapter one of *The Silver Chair*, too, he speaks dismissively of coeducational' schools where people who did 'horrid' things, or who were bullied, were referred to by the Head as interesting 'psychological cases' and would be talked to endlessly by the Head. If these children 'knew the right sort of thing to say to the Head, the main result was that you became rather a favourite than otherwise'. His opposition to such people reaches its zenith in the *Abolition of Man*, where the 'Clevers' are presented in terms of the modern educators who, in Lewis's view, tended to starve the sensibility of their pupils, thus making them 'easier prey to the propagandist when he comes'! Thus, he claimed, we 'make men without chests and expect of them virtue and enterprise. We laugh at honour and are shocked to find traitors in our midst. We castrate and bid the geldings be fruitful.'

The Pilgrim's Regress is important, too because of its detailed analysis of *Sehnsucht* (or Joy), which became a normative part of Lewis's whole thinking; it also crystallises his view of allegory and myth. Its relevance, too, for an age over fifty years on from the first publication can be shown in another way. Fashions – philosophical, political and sociological – and personalities have inevitably changed since 1933, but not the abiding significance of traditional Christianity for a world divided by ideological and economic barriers. Liberal theologians still inculcate the same bland assumptions, and claim that doubt – even of such cardinal doctrines of the faith as Christ's atoning death, the Virgin Birth, and the Resurrection – is a worthy, even a humble attitude. Lewis would have none of this. Equally, there are still people who view culture and reason as dangerous enemies. To all such over-emphases or mis-placed enthusiasms *The Pilgrim's Regress* is a powerful antidote and corrective, and it deserves to be re-discovered and enjoyed. It does not – it must be admitted – yield its pearls easily, and there are places where Lewis is either too heavy or too complex, but it does repay the discriminating and persevering reader.

One other point: in spite of its lack of commercial success, and the comparative neglect even by devoted Lewis readers, it was this work which launched him into the world of the professional theologian, because it brought him to the attention of Dr Alex Vidler,[36] then editor of the monthly journal, *Theology*. He wanted to develop some 'literary interest' in the journal and invited Lewis to become a sort of literary 'collaborator' This invitation was accepted with alacrity and it led to some very lively and controversial exchanges of views in the pages of the magazine, including such notable papers as 'Christianity and Culture'.

CHAPTER FOUR

The Imaginative Apologist

Well over thirty years ago Professor Chad Walsh published a study of Lewis's works up to 1949, bearing the title *C. S. Lewis: Apostle to the Skeptics*. Clearly this volume, though valuable and constructive in many ways, is of limited value for readers mid-way through the nineteen eighties, simply because many works by or about Lewis have been written and published in the intervening years. But the title he adopted is arresting and significant and aptly summarises a fundamental and enduring aspect of Lewis's work, namely his rôle as a Christian apologist and commentator. Other related descriptions of him include, 'Defender of the Faith', 'Guru to earnest intellectuals seeking faith', and 'Unorthodox defender of the Orthodox', the first and last of which are in happy accord with Walsh's original description.

It is absolutely certain that Lewis himself would have eschewed all such labels – he preferred to describe himself simply as a Christian, although he would offer two further qualifications: one, that his Christianity was dogmatic and not tinged 'with Modernist reservations'; and two, that he was fully and completely committed to 'supernaturalism' in all its power and vigour.[1] Several deductions may be drawn from the above statements. It is patently obvious that he was no 'liberal' Christian[2]; and also that he was concerned with defending and expounding his understanding of historic Christianity, later dubbed by him 'Mere Christianity', by

51

which he meant pure Christianity. It is important to define carefully the word *apologist*. One possible way would be to consult the various dictionaries and lexicons, but perhaps it is more relevant and worthwhile for our purposes to seek for an answer from Lewis's own articles and published works. Although he never attempted to put forward a systematic account of his beliefs and theology – presumably because he did not consider it to be necessary – he has defined in a number of places what he understood by the term 'Christian apologetics'.

In 1945, for example, he read a paper to an assembly of Anglican priests and youth leaders of the Church in Wales at Carmarthen which bore precisely this title. In it he begins by interpreting 'apologetics' as a defence of Christianity, by which he meant the faith propounded by the original apostles, attested to by the martyrs of all ages, interpreted by the Fathers and embodied and exemplified theologically in the Creeds. As such, his model was not a particular form of personal religion, nor an individual emphasis, rather the foundation provided by the New Testament. He views the honest distinction between what the faith actually says and what people would have liked it to have said as being vitally important for the apologist's whole rôle and approach, simply because it is difficult to get a modern audience to appreciate that those who preach Christianity are doing so because they think it to be true, whereas most people think the preaching is being done for the good of society in general.[3]

This distinction helps in other ways too, simply because it makes clear to the people being addressed that what is being offered them is objective fact, not ideals, and certainly not 'viewpoints'. Such an approach also affects the apologist himself, in that it compels him to face up squarely and rigorously to aspects of original Christianity he may find obscure or objectionable. Nor can he ignore or skip or slide over what is disagreeable or unpopular. Progress in Christian knowledge and faith, Lewis believed, is achieved only by facing the very considerable challenge of the doctrines which are either 'difficult or repellant'.[4] In contrast to this, the tendency of liberal Christianity is to seek to alter or free itself from the perplexing parts of the truth. In Lewis's estimation this is only a recipe for stagnant or unsatisfactory Christianity.

Here we find Lewis's characteristic emphases. Christian apologetics is concerned with defending historic Christianity, not because it is good and pleasant and diverting, but because it is *true*. Consequently it is to be defended honestly – without spurious claims – and robustly, without glossing over the problems. The timeless truths of Christianity are the touchstones by which contemporary modes of thought, be they political, philosophical or scientific, are to be judged and evaluated: 'We must at all costs not move with the times'.[5] It is also Christianity with a strong supernatural content:[6] not for him a truncated or watered down version of the faith. In the same paper Lewis stresses that the very fact of being an apologist can have a detrimental effect on a person's own faith; the only antidote for this is for the apologist to stand back from the intellectual arguments and to seek and to desire Christ himself.[7]

He emphasised too that the apologist's arguments must be based on fact,[8] and must be presented with full intellectual and rational rigour.[9] In this process the intelligence is sharpened and made more incisive.[10] Lewis was equally adamant that the apologist should state his case in the particular language 'of our own age'.[11] To him clarity of presentation was of supreme importance; the language of the audience must be acquired. In order to substantiate his contentions he lists words which are used in different senses by the layman and the theologian (eighteen in all). Here is the first:

> *Atonement.* Does not really exist in a spoken modern English, though it would be recognized as "a religious word". In so far as it conveys any meaning to the uneducated I think it means *compensation.* No one word will express to them what Christians means by *Atonement*: you must paraphrase.[12]

He concludes this section by asserting that if an apologist or preacher finds himself unable to translate his thoughts or theology into 'uneducated' language, then he is probably confused in hs own mind and in his understanding of the concepts and ideas being discussed. Theology in the vernacular was Lewis's especial strength, and in his 1958 debate with Norman Pittenger he expressed himself with characteristic robustness: 'Any fool can write *learned* language. The vernacular is the real test. If you can't turn your faith into it, then either you don't understand it or you don't believe it'.[13] While not all would agree with this rather outspoken view, we would all agree that to be an effective tool for communication language must be precise and unequivocal[14] and uncluttered,[15] and certainly not over-technical or abstruse.[16]

It is also important to stress that Lewis was not concerned with defending any denominational or sectarian view of Christianity; he preferred to concentrate on what he called 'the enormous common ground'.[17] The bond between all believers is after Christianity, 'mere' Christianity,[18] the belief that has been the common inheritance of all Christians in all ages. Consequently, there were some disputed matters on which he maintained a discreet silence,[19] again an attitude he espoused because he was not expounding *his* form of religion, rather the traditional 'certitudes'[20] of the Christian faith.[21]

He also contended that, as opposed to yet more books about Christianity, what is required is 'more little books by Christians on other subjects – with their Christianity latent'.[22] Poetically he put his vision – at the same time his prayer – like this:

From all my lame defeats and oh! much more
From all the victories that I seemed to score;
From cleverness shot forth on Thy behalf
At which, while angels weep, the audience laugh;
From all my proofs of Thy divinity,
Thou, who wouldst give no sign, deliver me.

Thoughts are but coins. Let me not trust, instead
Of Thee, their thin-worn image of Thy head.
From all my thoughts, even from my thoughts of Thee,
O thou fair Silence, fall, and set me free.

Lord of the narrow gate and the needle's eye,
Take from me all my trumpery lest I die.[23]

Inevitably the task he set himself led to controversy, both orally and in print. To it he brought many gifts: immense learning, a brilliantly analytical mind, a creative imagination allied to reason, much common sense, and an incomparable dialectical skill. He discharged his task so successfully that before the end of the nineteen forties he had become, without question, the most famous and popular spokesman for Christianity throughout the English-speaking world.[24] How right he was to confine himself to the prime features of the faith, for by so doing he won the respect − albeit grudgingly at times − of Christians of all shades of opinions. His religious works also gained acceptance with a large number of sceptics, who admired his urbane wit, wisdom, and inexorable logic. In America his impact was just as great as in Britain because he provided 'orthodoxy' and not 'obscurantist fundamentalism' (Chad Walsh). People who were searching for faith found that Lewis's brand of historic Christianity violated neither their intellect nor their knowledge.

Lewis's apologetic work was diverse and varied.

1. Exposition and Defence

One of the apologist's prime functions is to set out Christian beliefs clearly and to defend them against other viewpoints. Lewis attempted this in *Mere Christianity*, *The Problem of Pain* and *Miracles*, although there is a sense in which the last name is a work of 'pure' theology.

Here we shall pay most attention to *Mere Christianity*, the content of which was first delivered as talks for BBC radio, then published in separate parts as *Broadcast Talks* (1942), *Christian Behaviour* (1943), and *Beyond Personality* (1944). For the sake of clarity − and brevity − what Lewis had to say may be grouped under a number of convenient − though admittedly arbitrary − headings:

(a) *The Law of Human Nature*

Lewis's intention in the first talk is two-fold. Firstly, it is to show that people all over the world have a 'curious idea' that they ought to behave in a certain way; and secondly that they do not live up to this known standard of behaviour which Lewis calls *The Law of Human Nature* (alternatively, the *Rule of Decent Behaviour*, or the *Moral Law*). He sees these two facts as being the foundation of all clear thinking about ourselves and the world in which we live.

The Moral Law is that which governs and directs a person's instincts; it is not the instincts themselves, nor merely social convention, nor the herd instinct. He gives various examples to justify this assertion. One of them poses the hypothetical situation of a person hearing a cry from a man in danger. It is possible to feel several different reactions at this point: to help (to assist the 'herd'), or, by contrast, to keep out of danger (self-preservation). Yet a third, however, tells the person to suppress the impulse to retreat from the scene of the potential danger.[25] That which helps us to evaluate the two instincts and decides which one is to be fostered is the Moral Law. This moral law is the standard against which conflicting impulses can be judged and evaluated; it is utterly above and beyond the facts of human behaviour. Consequently it has something of radical importance to tell us about the world we live in.

Essentially, Lewis says, there are three main views about the universe. One sees space and matter as purely chance happenings, a hit-or-miss affair, a sort of fluke,[26] from which human kind has developed as a result of a series of blind chances. Opposed to this materialist view is the religious viewpoint: that behind the universe there is a purposeful, conscious, and selective mind.[27] To accept the first of these alternatives is to believe that there is no power or reason behind the universe; to adopt the second is accept the activity of a controlling power behind the universe. The crucial question is what happens when the packet called Man is investigated. Lewis argues that when this is done we find that man does not exist on his own, that he is under a law, requiring him to act and behave in a certain manner.[28]

Somebody is apparently directing the universe. He is a great artist and also quite inflexible. He has put a moral law into our hearts, a standard of absolute goodness.[29]   The above is a bare summary of the argument that Lewis set out in impressive detail. He did so precisely because 'Christianity does not make sense until you have faced the sort of facts I have been describing'.[30] His argument is not unduly technical or abstruse; in fact, he roots his examples in the realities and awkwardnesses of everyday experience. Ultimately he did so because he wanted his readers to find *truth*.

(b) *The Key to History*

Lewis sees this question as closely linked to the sort of God people believe in.[31] Either he is 'beyond good and evil' or he is quite specifically 'good' or 'righteous'. If, however, he is a good God, why has the world he made gone so drastically wrong? Rejecting the atheistic view, and also the 'idealist' view that everything is as it should be with no need for doctrines such as sin and hell, Lewis argues that the only clue to the present state of evil in the universe is that 'an evil power has made Himself for the present the Prince of this World'.[32] This at once raises the problem of free will, which made evil possible. But Lewis, with the poet John Milton, sees no problem here because free will, while making evil a possibility, is also the only thing that brings about the possibility of joy or goodness or love.[33] To ask God to bestow happiness upon us without our bothering about 'religion' is futile: he cannot do this without giving us himself.[34] This, in Lewis's mind, is the key to history, and it leads on inevitably to the subject of the third section.

(c) *The Atonement*

Lewis refutes the patronising nonsense of regarding Jesus as a great moral teacher. He is either the Son of God, as he claimed, or he is deluded or worse.[35] He came to this world, in a very real sense enemy territory, in order to die, which is precisely the point in history 'at which something absolutely unimaginable from outside shows through into our own world'. Lewis does not speculate, however, on *how* Christ's death has put man right with God. To him it is quite simply part of the 'mystery of the Gospel'[36]; all we know is that Christ's atoning death – a fundamental postulate of the Christian faith – gives man a new start.[37] Alongside this there is the need for repentance: it is a repentance which leads to the death of all our self-conceit, self-will; it means killing off part of our selves.[38] What is involved is not mere cosmetic adjustment, rather willing submission to God's will.

(d) *Christian Morality*

To Lewis, morality is not a meddlesome or interfering influence but simply rules or guidelines for the proper running of the 'human machine'. As such it is concerned with the way people treat each other, and thus with the notions of fair play, balance, and harmony. Ultimately it is bound up with the whole purpose of life itself. Of course he is primarily interested in Christian morality. Christ did not come to earth to preach a new morality; Christianity does not offer any political programme which is at all comprehensive or detailed; and a Christian society will never arrive until the vast majority of people 'really want it'.[39] Later in the same section ('Social Morality') he says that bringing this about is the responsibility of the layman: the applying of truly Christian principles must be the rôle of the trade union member on the shop floor, the schoolmaster in the study and classroom, and of novelists and dramatists who are convinced about their faith and employ their creative gifts to share it with other people.[40]

Christian morality includes patience, temperance, charity, Christian marriage (for life), willingness to forgive, and the avoidance of pride, which he saw as the 'great' sin.

(e) *Some Theological Virtues*

The first of these is *hope*. One of the 'theological' virtues, it is not a form of escapism, nor does it require that Christians ignore the present world – in fact, as he points out, the Christians who did most for the present world were those who thought most of the next. Indeed, it is because Christians have largely stopped thinking about the world to come that they have become so ineffective in this world.[41]

The second virtue he describes is *faith*, which to Lewis means essentially two things. There is belief: assuming the cardinal doctrines of Christianity to be true. Then there is faith in a practical sense: a person's own efforts are not sufficient; he must be enveloped by and depend upon Christ's indwelling power and strength. This is another way of saying that Christ imparts to us 'sonship' as Christians: it is at once a great dignity and a great responsibility.

(f) *The Doctrine of the Trinity*

This is examined in Book Four of *Mere Christianity*. To Lewis, theology was of prime importance and above all practical; thus to reject or neglect theology results in hopelessly inadequate ideas about God. He distinguishes beween 'begetting' and 'making': a man begets a child but makes an ornament. Similarly 'God' begets 'Christ' but 'makes' a man, and what God begets is something of the 'same kind' as himself.[42] Then he points out what he calls the most important difference between Christianity and all other religions: that in Christianity God is not a mute or static force, not even a person. He is 'a dynamic, pulsating activity, a life'. The importance of this is paramount, because Christianity is all about the possibility of sharing God's life, becoming a son of God, allowing the Holy Spirit to mould and modify one's thinking, in short becoming what Lewis graphically calls 'a little Christ'.[43] When we pray, the Son of God injects his thoughts into us begetting himself in us; it is the giving up of our 'self' to him, and he advises:

> Keep back nothing. Nothing that you have not given away will ever be really yours. Nothing in you that has not died will ever be raised from the dead. Look for yourself, and you will find in the long run only hatred, loneliness, despair, rage, ruin, and decay. But look for Christ and you will find Him, and with Him everything else thrown in.[44]

Mere Christianity is an amalgam of conservative and controversial teaching. The former includes the following emphases: the existence of the law of Human Nature; the fact of sin and its pernicious effects both in nature and in man; Christ's redemptive or atoning death; the obligation to live in a new way after becoming a Christian; that God requires not fine feelings or exalted insights alone, but Christ-like conduct.

More controversial are his refusal to theorise on precisely how Christ's death puts a man right with God; his view that 'there are three things that spread the life of Christ to us: baptism, belief, and that mysterious action which different Christians call by different names – Holy Communion, the Mass, the Lord's Supper';[45] his contention that it is unreasonable to think of the world as falling into two – and only two – sections, Christian and non-Christian, his reason being that the world is simply not sub-divided into those who are one hundred percent non-Christians and others who are one hundred percent Christians – there are others who are in the slow process of becoming Christians.[46] Correspondence following the original broadcasts made it clear that some of these views were unacceptable to dogmatic evangelicals and others to dogmatic catholics but on the central doctrines of Christianity Lewis stands firm; a most formidable advocate.

Difficulties are not avoided; they are faced honestly, rationally, with careful and lucid arguments. To all these strengths be added a fertile imagination; he had the rare gift of being able to make righteousness readable'. Its stimulating, unfailingly robust and logical defence of historic Christianity makes *Mere Christianity* a most significant work. Its style is remarkable for variety, lucidity, and simplicity. Lewis knows how to capture the attention of his audience by placing what he has to say firmly within their experience. He knew how ordinary people felt and thought – and was able to portray their feelings, failings and hopes, accurately, crisply, and aptly. The same effect is achieved in *The Screwtape Letters*.

Many people in the nineteen forties were disillusioned with what Wain describes as an 'anti-clerical and rationalistic left-wing generation', and were looking for an uncluttered, reasonable, and robust faith, which they found in Lewis.

It is against this social, religious and cultural background that we must also place *The Problem of Pain* (1940) and *The Screwtape Letters* (1942) – two of Lewis's most famous and best-selling books – which made him widely known as a writer on Christian and ethical matters. In the former he deals with one of the most fundamental and contentions of all issues connected with the Christian faith, namely the apparent contradiction between a good, powerful and loving God and the existence of wide-spread suffering in his world.

His treatment of the subject is thorough, as the headings of the major chapters indicate: 'Divine Omnipotence', 'Divine Goodness', 'Human Wickedness', 'The Fall of Man', 'Human Pain', 'Hell', 'Animal Pain', and 'Heaven'.

The Problem of Pain is packed with theology. Perhaps the best gloss on its central argument is found in a letter Lewis wrote to Arthur Greeves on 6th July 1949:

I do *not* hold that God 'sends' sickness or war in the sense in which He sends us all good things. Hence in Luke xiii.16 Our Lord clearly attributes a disease not to the action of His Father but to that of Satan. I think you are quite right. All suffering arises from sin.

The sense in which it is also God's will seems to me twofold (a) The one you mention: that God willed the free will of men and angels in spite of His knowledge that it cd. lead in some cases to sin and thence to suffering: i.e. He thought Freedom worth creating even at that price. It is like when a mother allows a small child to walk on its own instead of holding it by her hand. She knows it may fall, but learning to walk on one's own is worth a few falls. When it does fall this is in one sense contrary to the mother's will: but the general situation in wh. falls are possible *is* the mother's will. (In fact, as you and I have so often said before 'in one way it is, in another way it isn't!') (b) The world is so made that the sins of one inflict suffering on another. Now I don't think God allows this to happen at random. I think that if He knew that the suffering entailed on innocent A by the sins of B wd. be (in the deep sense & the long run) *bad* for A, He wd. shield A from it. And in that sense I think it is sometimes God's will that A should go through this suffering. The supreme case is the suffering that *our* sins entailed on Christ. When Christ saw that suffering drawing near He prayed (Luke xxii.42) 'If thou be willing, remove this cup from me: nevertheless not my will but thine.' This seems to me to make it quite clear that the crucifixion was (in the very qualified sense wh. I've tried to define) God's will. I do not regard myself as disagreeing with you, but as holding the same view with a few necessary complications which you have omitted.[47]

Lewis recognises too that there is no easy solution to the problem of pain, and that no intellectual solution or formula can do away with the need for patience, fortitude and courage.

Though well-received by the reviewers, *The Problem of Pain* is not generally regarded as Lewis's best theological work, but it did have one particularly important effect in that it brought him to the attention of the B.B.C., leading eventually to the phenomenal success of the broadcast talks now collected together as *Mere Christianity*.

Lewis's popularity reached even greater heights with the publication, in weekly instalments in the *Manchester Guardian* between 2nd May and 28th November 1941, of thirty-one letters written by an old devil to a young devil on the art of temptation. First published as a book in February 1942, *The Screwtape Letters* proved to be a great commercial success, being reprinted eight times before the end of 1942. The paperback edition has sold over one million copies in England and America. By now Lewis was an international figure: the imaginative apologist had become 'Everyman's theologian'.

2. Presenting Christian Doctrine

Relating to the works discussed above, which are properly speaking apologetic, are other books in which Lewis presents Christian doctine clearly and compellingly, sometimes pre-empting, but not as a rule opposing, alternative viewpoints.

In this category we may include *The Great Divorce*. In this book, published in 1945, Lewis once more utilises allegory. The title derives from Blake's work, *The Marriage of Heaven and Hell*. Lewis believes that such a marriage is impossible. It is impossible that any process of 'mere development or adjustment or refinement will somehow turn evil into good without our being called on for a final and total rejection of anything we should like to retain'. In the allegory, a number of people take a day trip from Hell to the borders of Heaven. As he shows how most of them refuse to stay in Heaven, Lewis develops one of his most characteristic themes – the total difference between evil and good. He made it clear that the last thing he wanted to do was to 'arouse curiosity about the details of the after-world'; nevertheless, the book contains a great deal of provocative and constructive thought about a traditional Christian doctrine.

Here too we encounter Lewis's detestation of all attempts to dilute or distort 'mere' Christianity. One of the characters is an apostate bishop who is an exponent of liberal Christianity. He derides as narrow-minded any belief in a literal Hell and Heaven since he is willing to accept their existence only in a spiritual sense. He is looking for 'the kingdom' but it is a kingdom in a carefully divined and limited sense: 'nothing superstitious or mythological.'[48]

The significance of *The Great Divorce* goes beyond its apologetic content and value. Here Lewis uses his familiarity with mediaeval allegory and myth in order to present theological ideas in an interesting and imaginative manner. Some critics criticise it as less witty than *The*

Screwtape Letters, but it presents many of Lewis's 'distinctives' in a highly effective way. Myth is seen as pointing beyond itself to a greater reality rather than being a mere figure of speech; there are no alternatives to Jesus Christ; Christianity is both a thoroughly supernatural faith and at the same time a radical process in which its adherents are progressively transformed by the renewing of their minds (Romans 12:2); the choices we make in life have eternal consequences.

The continuing relevance of *The Great Divorce* during the nineteeen eighties cannot be doubted – not only does Lewis expose liberal theologians who claim to value Christianity but who reject the resurrection because it is unacceptable to them – it also illustrates the satanic way in which ordinary people may have their minds ensnared and prefer illusion to the reality (in this case of Heaven) offered by Jesus Christ.

The Resurrection too had been rejected when it 'ceased to commend itself' to the Bishop's God-given 'critical faculties'. The reference to 'critical faculties' is an important part of the clergyman's desire to appear as a man of scrupulous intellectual honesty, and it can be compared with other expressions of a similar tone – on page 36, reacting to the word 'Hell' he says, 'There is no need to be profane, my dear boy. I may not be very orthodox, in your sense of the word, but I do feel that these matters ought to be discussed simply, and seriously and reverently.' Later he opines: 'There is hide-bound prejudice, and intellectual dishonesty, and timidity, and stagnation. But honest opinions fearlessly followed – they are not sins' (page 37). The truth is that such doctrines as the Resurrection were rejected by the bishop in order to gain popularity and to further his career; not for him the 'crude salvationism' propounded by others; he had been 'afraid of a breach with the spirit of the age, afraid of ridicule, afraid (above all) of real spiritual fears and hopes'.[49] When invited, 'in sight of heaven' to repent and believe, the apostate clergyman replies, 'But my dear boy, I believe already. We may not be perfectly agreed, but you have completely misjudged me if you do not realise that my religion is a very real and a very precious thing to me'.[50] In the after-life he seeks 'a wider sphere of usefulness – and scope for the talents that God has given me – and an atmosphere of free enquiry – in short, all that one means by civilisation and – er – the spiritual life'.[51] He is told however that he cannot be promised any of these things: 'No sphere of usefulness: you are not needed there at all! No scope for your talents: only forgiveness for having perverted them'.[52] He refuses the option of heaven, and in a final speech applauds the pathway of duty, describing the paper he is about to give at a Theological Society on how Jesus, in maturity, outgrew his earlier views. What precisely is meant by this, or the enigmatic assertion that such a shift in the balance of his opinions 'deepens the significance of the Crucifixion' is far from clear.[53] His attitude contrasts with Lewis's unswerving belief in Heaven, the realm of the pure 'in Christ', for, as he says, only they will desire to see God. Lewis conceived of heaven as the 'home for humanity and therefore contains all that is implied in a glorified life'. He was equally adamant in his belief in Hell, in a physical Resurrection, and the Supernatural.

Another character who may be linked with Mr Broad is the Vicar in *The Screwtape Letters*. He has so diluted the faith in order to palliate the apparent unbelief of his congregation, that he now appals them with his unbelief; he has become an abject and pitiable character whose reading revolves round 'his fifteen favourite psalms and twenty favourite lessons'.[54] Lewis was deeply out of sympathy with people such as the Bishop and the Vicar. At times he expressed his bafflement with a world that had become 'simply too much for people' like himself and his brother whom he portrayed as being 'the old square-rigged type'.[55] At times this bafflement became downright annoyance, even anger on other occasions.[56]

Another book in which Christian doctrine is described is *The Four Loves*. It is not among Lewis's outstanding achievements but it was the first of his books that I ever read. I was sufficiently attracted by it to go on to read the others.

After differentiating between Gift-love (a typical example 'would be that love which moves a man to work and plan and save for the future well-being of his family which he will die without sharing or seeing') and Need-love ('that which sends a lonely or frightened child to its mother's arms'), Lewis examines each of the four loves: (1) *Affection* (Greek *storge*), which includes both Gift and Need-love. It has to do with the affection of parents for children and vice-versa. King Lear provides an apposite example at the beginning of the play of that name ('a very unlovable old man devoured with a ravenous appetite for Affection'). (2) *Friendship*. This love was fully appreciated by the Ancients, but tends to be ignored by the modern world. (3) *Eros* is the state of 'being in love'. In essence Lewis's enquiry is concerned not with that sexuality which is common to humans *and* beasts, but with 'one uniquely human variation of it which develops within "love". ... The carnal or animally sexually element within Eros.' He also describes it as 'Venus', – what is known to be sexual by those who experience it; what could be proved to be sexual by the simplest observations'. (4) *Charity* is completely different from all natural and human loves. To understand this love we must begin with 'God is love'. It is God, as Creator of Nature, who 'implements in us both Gift-loves and Need-loves. The crux of the chapter on charity is Lewis's argument that, in addition to the 'natural' loves, God can impart an even greater love: *agape* love, self-giving and totally un-selfish, thinking only of the good of other people.

Many writers – including Ovid, St Bernard, the Apostle Paul, and Stendhal – have examined different aspects of affection, friendship, eros and charity, but without present-ing as cohesive a view of the anatomy of love as Lewis does in this book. He is particularly effective on the distortions which can cause the first three to be perverted and even dangerous.

Doubtless some readers and commentators will cavil at the thought of the Narnia Chronicles being viewed as 'concealed apologetics', but there is quite explicit evidence to sustain such an approach to the stories which have enchanted children and adults ever since they first appeared. In the volume entitled *Christian Apologetics*, Lewis says that what is required is not more books about Christ-ianity but books by Christians on other subjects, with their

Christianity latent. In *Mere Christianity* he observes that 'Christian literature comes from Christian novelists and dramatists'. Here is the truth about the Narnia Chronicles: they are the work of a convinced Christian, with a highly imaginative mind, who wrote stories: no more, no less. Certainly we know that Lewis never set out to incorporate theological ideas or subjects in an explicit way. To have done so would have resulted in a stereotyped and theoretical tone, and would have damaged the chronicles as stories. In *Of Other Worlds*, Lewis denies the accusation that he began by asking himself how he could say something about Christianity to children; chose the fairy tale as a suitable genre; assembled information about child psychology and decided upon the particular age group to aim for; then finally listed the basic Christian truths and constructed allegories embodying them. His purpose in fact was to strip these stories of any 'stained-glass and Sunday School associations'.[57]

Representations of Christian principles or correspondence of Christian characters are there, but only unconsciously, for Lewis's method is entirely natural; the result is both enjoyment and instruction. He explained his position to the Milton Society in America: 'The fairy tale was the genre best fitted for what I wanted to say.' In another letter, this time to a young admirer, he said:

I'm not exactly 'representing' the real (Christian) story in symbols. I'm more saying, 'Suppose there were a world like Narnia and it needed rescuing and the Son of God (or the Great Emperor-Over-Sea) went to redeem *it*, as He came to redeem ours, what might it, that world, all have been like?'[59]

Thus it was with creative imagination foremost and with pictures in his mind that Lewis wrote the Narnia Chronicles. The sequence of the stories – not the order of publication – is as follows: *The Magician's Nephew* (1955); *The Lion, the Witch and the Wardrobe* (1950); *The Horse and His Boy* (1954); *Prince Caspian* (1951); *The Voyage of the 'Dawn Treader'* (1952); *The Silver Chair* (1953); *The Last Battle* (1956).

As an example of the Narnia books, we consider the first of them to be published, namely *The Lion, the Witch and the Wardrobe*, in which the events related take place a thousand Narnian years after the original creation of Narnia, which would correspond to the year 1940 in England (that is, forty years after the occurrences in *The Magician's Nephew*).

First, then, the framework of the story. Forced to leave London by the war, Peter, Edmund, Susan and Lucy live with Professor Kirke ('a very old man with shaggy white hair which grew over most of his face as well as his head') in a very large country house, which was 'complicated and full of hiding-places'. Their adventure begins when they decide to explore the house. They discover a wardrobe, which turns out to be the doorway to Narnia itself, where they encounter Mr Tumnus. He is supposed to hand over any Son of Adam or Daughter of Eve found in the wood to the Witch Jadis, but he allows Lucy to return to the others. Later all four children enter the wardrobe, though Peter is sceptical, claiming it is all nonsense,[60] His mood, however, changes later to something akin to exhilaration, as he realises that they are, after all, in Lucy's wood.

Jadis is Queen of Narnia where her spells have ensured that it is 'always winter ... never Christmas'. The only hope for the oppressed inhabitants of Narnia lies in the return of the Lion, Aslan. When Edmund, who takes the Witch's side, gives her the news of Aslan's arrival in Narnia she makes him prisoner and hastens through the thawing forests to the Stern Table. Here Aslan and the Witch confront each other while the children look on. The Witch claims, firstly, that Edmund is a traitor, and secondly, that as she has lawful authority over him, she has a right to kill him. However, it is Aslan who dies in Edmund's place, amidst the abuse and derision of his enemies.

But this is not the end. Aslan returns to life, frees the 'statues' of people who have been frozen by the Witch, then defeats her and her ghastly followers in a dramatic battle. The story ends with Peter as High King of Narnia, the others ruling with him as Kings and Queens. The ancient prophecy has been fulfilled:

'When Adam's flesh and Adam's bone
Sits at Cair Paravel in throne,
The evil time will be over and done.'

The story is dominated by Aslan, the lion, who is designated as the 'Lord of the whole wood', 'the King', 'the great Emperor beyond-the-sea', and 'the King of the Beasts'.

Apart from natural symbolism, the lion has an important place in Christian imagery. Thus in the Old Testament, the nation of Israel is likened to a 'lion's whelp' (Genesis 49:9). The Psalmist fears that his persecutor will tear his soul 'like a lion' (Psalm 7:2), while Isaiah has a vision of God's future kingdom when the 'wolf and the lion' shall be tamed and (Isaiah 11:6) The New Testament too contains significant references to the lion. Peter exhorts his readers to be sober and vigilant because they face an adversary who is portrayed as a 'roaring lion' (1 Peter 5:8), while John, the Seer, is told by one of the Elders not to weep, since 'the Lion of the tribe of Judah' is going to triumph in a display of mighty strength and universal authority. In the same chapter the Lion (Christ) is also the Lamb, combining power with gentler qualities. Echoes of Christ-likeness are found in Aslan. He is the only source of help for the children, and his rich, deep voice 'took the fidgets out of them. They now felt glad and quiet and it didn't seem awkward to them to stand and say nothing' – they are comforted and re-assured by Aslan's presence. He is one too whose prophecies are vindicated – for example, he prophesies that Peter will sit in Cair Paravel as 'the High King over all the rest'. He dies instead of Edmund (and only for him), but returns victorious and triumphant. All this reminds us of Jesus Christ, and certainly Lewis meant us to view Aslan as a divine being, not, as he says in one of his letters, as simply an allegorical figure. Aslan's death, like Christ's, is sacrificial and redemptive.

Roger Lancelyn Green comments:

it was natural that the world of Narnia should fit into the over-all Christian universe in which he believed so wholeheartedly – and that Aslan should represent Christ. But this is only an added dimension to the stories: if you are to realize it at all you should do so without being told what to look out for – and if you do not realize it, you will enjoy the stories just as much, for they are superb adventure sories in their own right, just as exciting for readers of a different religion, or of no religion at all.[61]

Whether our reaction to Aslan is religious or not, his presence pervades and dominates the whole book. Similarly, the Law of Deep Magic also functions at two levels. In response to Aslan's request, 'Tell us of the Deep Magic', the Witch replies that all traitors belong to her and that she has the power of life or death over them. Obviously this is reminiscent of the crushing rigidity of God's law, as seen in the Old Testament, thundering and dreadful, but it does not matter if a reader fails to make this connection, because the requirements of the Law of Deep Magic lead to the violent death of Aslan, itself an integral part of the overall story.

Again, certain details of the story remind us of fundamental Christian concepts. The breaking of the Stone, for example, brings to mind the veil of the Temple being torn in two (Matthew 27:51) when Christ was dying; Aslan too like Christ was really alive in spite of having been killed (Matthew 28:6). He received the joyous adoration and kisses of Lucy and Susan, just as Christ received those of the women in the incident recorded in John 20.

The Lion, the Witch and Wardrobe may be read as a first-rate story of magical, mysterious and enchanting adventure, still popular today, enjoyed not only by children but also by adults. At the same time it includes details and matters which may be related easily and unobtrusively to those things which are a permanent and abiding part of the Christian story.

Even if the link between Aslan's death and Christ's death is not made, the narrative reads well and convincingly, and on a purely human and artistic level the reader, through the reactions of Lucy and Susan, is involved with Aslan's suffering, and is horrified and appalled by the multiple indignities heaped upon him; the reader feels the Witch's intense hatred towards Aslan, and that while her ostensible reason for killing him is to appease the apparently righteous and legal demands of the Law of Deep Magic, she is in fact more interested in the act of killing itself and is enjoying it in a way that reveals her loathsome and hateful personality. Our sympathy is evoked by the deep devotion of Lucy and Susan, who express their impotence in the face of such cruelty: '"Oh how *can* they?", said Lucy, tears streaming down her cheeks. "The brutes, the brutes!"'. Literary felicity and Christian symbolism blend together in a work of considerable charm.

Undoubtedly one of the reasons he was so successful as an apologist was that he had this gift for presenting a doctrine in such a way that the reader is disarmed and led step by step – even without overt argument – into saying, 'Why, it does make sense after all!'

3 Polemic

There is another related element in his writing which is merely polemic. This is present to a certain extent in *The Pilgrim's Regress* where Lewis's attack on 'liberal' or 'enlightened' Christianity is found in his portrayal of Mr Broad, whom John, the hero of *The Pilgrim's Regress*, encounters after having met Mr Enlightenment, Mr Neo-Classical, and the Clevers.

John seeks specific directions regarding the continuance of his journey, especially whether it is obligatory to cross the canyon. Mr Broad at first comments on the danger of making these matters, in his own words, 'too definite'. Later he concludes with the vague statement that great truths must be 're-interpreted' in each and every age. John is unhappy with Mr Broad's reply, but insists that he must find the Island.[62] In general we notice a marked contrast between John's intensity and Mr Broad's genial (but ineffectual) affability, which is, in reality, only a cover for his indecisiveness.[63] More specifically, Mr Broad eschews what he describes as 'mere orthodoxy';[64] it is worth recalling at this point Screwtape's advice to Wormwood to encourage doctrinal lukewarmness if at all possible. Mr Broad is bland, evasive, imprecise and vapid. He may be compared with the 'Bright Person' in *The Great Divorce*.

In contrast, Lewis's attitude is that personal responsibility culminating in a choice is a *norm* of Christian experience: it must not ever be obscured by the use of language such as that deployed by Mr Broad and others like him. What John patently required, and what Mr Broad was unable to provide, was a detailed directive which would inspire confidence and assurance. By contrast, Mr Broad's words make John feel increasingly unsure,[65] though he still maintains: 'I want my Island.'

This polemic element is also seen very clearly in *The Abolition of Man* and in a paper entitled 'Modern Theology and Biblical Criticism,'[66] recently re-published as 'Fern-Seed and Elephants',[67] which was read originally to the students of Westcott House, a Cambridge theological college, on 11th May 1959. This attack is not on unbelievers but on liberal biblical scholarship. Lewis begins characteristically by detaching and distancing himself from the theologically trained students in his audience, referring to himself as an outsider, though he reminds them that it is precisely the outsiders with whom they as clergy will have to deal on a regular basis. He defines the 'outsider' with care: as either an uneducated person himself; or an educated person who has not been educated theologically. He emphasises that a theology which denies the historicity of those facets which Christians have always believed implicitly – for example, the miracles and the Resurrection – will not be recognised by the uneducated person as Christianity at all. The main part of the paper, however, is occupied with an account of Lewis's reactions to such a theology – or to use the metaphor he utilised, the advice of a sheep telling shepherds things which only a sheep can tell them. His 'bleating' contains four essential points.

The first is that the undermining of the old orthodoxy has been done by New Testament critics whose literary judgment Lewis distrusts. He doubts their perception of the texts they are reading, but most damagingly he thinks they lack literary judgment itself. He cites the influential New Testament scholar, Rudolf Bultmann:

> 'The personality of Jesus has no importance for the kerygma either of Paul or of John ... Indeed the tradition of the earliest Church did not even unconsciously preserve a picture of his personality. Every attempt to reconstruct one remains a play of subjective imagination.[68]

Responding to Bultmann's assertion that the New Testament does not preserve Our Lord's personality, Lewis distinguishes between different types of character. On the one hand, there are historical characters of whom we feel we have no personal knowledge (e.g. Alexander). On the other hand, there are those who cannot claim any historical reality but who are nevertheless 'real', for example, Mr Pickwick or Falstaff. He claims that there are only three characters who lay claim to the first type of reality but who actually have the second sort as well. They are Plato's Socrates, the Jesus of the Gospels, and Boswell's Johnson. As far as Jesus is concerned, he concludes that even those passages which are primarily 'concerned with the divine, and least with the human nature, bring us face to face with the personality'.[69]

His second 'bleat' is about liberal theology's assumption that very soon the real behaviour, purpose, and teaching of Jesus came to be both misunderstood and misrepresented by his followers, but that modern scholars have been able to recover the truth about all of these. This claim is vigorously demolished:

> The idea that any man or writer should be opaque to those who lived in the same culture, spoke the same language, shared the same habitual imagery and unconscious assumptions, and yet be transparent to those who have none of these advantages, is in my opinion preposterous. There is an *a priori* improbability in it which almost almost no argument and no evidence could counterbalance.[71]

The third 'bleat' is Lewis's familiar objection to the efforts of many liberal theologians to exclude the supernatural from Christianity. Such a view is based on an *a priori* belief that

'inspired prediction can never occur'. 'The rejection as unhistorical of all passages which narrate miracles is sensible [only] if we start by knowing that the miraculous in general never occurs'.[72]
His fourth 'bleat' is about the attempts of liberal criticism

> to reconstruct the genesis of the texts it studies; what vanished documents each author used, when and where he wrote, with what purposes, under what influences – the whole *Sitz im Leben* of the text.[73]

He refutes this by recounting an experience early in his career:

> I had published a book of essays; and the one into which I had put most of my heart, the one I really cared about and in which I discharged a keen enthusiasm, was on William Morris. And in almost the first review I was told that this was obviously the only one in the book in which I had felt no interest. Now don't mistake. The critic was, I now believe, quite right in thinking it the worst essay in the book; at least everyone agreed with him. Where he was totally wrong was in his imaginary history of the causes which produced its dullness.[74]

Finally he points out how important it is for the clergy to hear what the laity are thinking; failure to do so will mean a shortening in the life-expectancy of the Church of England.[75] Dr Austen Farrer regarded this paper as the best thing Lewis ever wrote: it is a succinct, carefully thought out indictment of modern theological trends; it presents a powerful case for historic Christianity. It is all the more impressive and devastating because it deals with the postulates of liberal theology on the basis of his own special expertise as a literary critic. Written with his usual economy and precision, this paper shows Lewis's ability to expose the heart of a problem. He pinpoints in particular the dilemma of the layman who is confronted by a theology which denies the historicity of almost everything in the biblical narratives to which Christian 'affections and thought' have been fixed. 'It will make him a Roman Catholic or an atheist. What you offer him he will not recognise as Christianity'.[76]

4. A General Comment

Lewis's output as an apologist was immense, a fact which is all the more remarkable when it is remembered that all the articles and books on religious topics were achieved in the midst of, and in addition to, his professional work at Oxford and Cambridge. Clearly enormous demands were made on his time – preparing students for public examinations, lecturing, writing on literary subjects, reviewing, etc. – so that he must have husbanded his time carefully. Indeed John Lawlor[77], who was tutored by Lewis in the nineteen thirties, says that he 'valued time as few men I have met, before or since, have done': 'After an early breakfast and a walk, nine o'clock in Term time would see him seated at his writing-table, wooden penholder and steel nib moving steadily over the page until the ten o'clock pupil knocked on his door.' This unremitting 'silent industry' was maintained throughout his life. His last article, 'We Have No "Right to Happiness"' was written in October 1963, just one month before he died.

It would be idle to pretend that his theological – in particular his apologetic – output was to everyone's liking. His fellow dons at Oxford resented his rôle as a 'popularizer of Christian dogma', and his standing as a scholar (which nobody seriously doubted) was 'checkmated by his unwelcome fame as an apologist of Christianity'; certainly this ambivalence was a factor in his never being rewarded with a professorial chair at Oxford. Mistrust, suspicion and jealousy all conspired to keep him from a prize he richly deserved, and when offered the new Chair of Medieval and Renaissance English at Cambridge, he accepted without any feelings of disloyalty (in 1954); later he turned down the Merton Professorship at Oxford (in 1957).

If it is a fact that the members of the academic community at Oxford were suspicious about the nature of his international fame, it is no less true that Lewis was the most powerful, persuasive and effective apologist for Christianity in the nineteen forties and fifties, with an influence and a reputation which extended far beyond Oxford – and in particular to America, where his standing today in the nineteen eighties probably exceeds his status in Britain.

The reasons for this astounding success, which he often found embarrassing, were many and varied, that is apart from the intrinsic quality and appeal of his published works. The nineteen forties and fifties, during which the stresses of war were succeeded by post-war austerity, had left many people with hopes shattered and with little prospect of any quick or easy solution to their problems. A sense of 'crisis and suffering' pervaded Britain and men and women were searching for an ethic or an ideology which would provide them with certainty, fixed standards and, perhaps most important of all, a reassuring hope for the future. All these were accessible in Lewis's response to religious questions. Disenchantment with the war and its aftermath will have been a factor in conditioning the minds of people, even though the pre-war years had seen the beginning of a decline in church/chapel attendance. Lewis's works appealed to men and women who, though they varied in class, education and wealth – found themselves in a 'waste land', facing

'A heap of broken images, where the sun beats
And the dead tree gives no shelter, the cricket no relief,
And the dry stone no sound of water'. (T. S. Eliot)

In such a setting, his books were refreshingly warm, personal, direct and positive. Intellectually too the climate was 'right' for his particular brand of reasoning and appeal. At Oxford Christianity was admired not only because of Lewis's robust dialectical approach, but because of the growing influence of T. S. Eliot's *Four Quartets*.[78]

Published in New York in 1943 (London in 1944), it consisted of four poems each of which had appeared separately: *Burnt Norton*, 1936; *East Coker*, 1940; *The Dry Salvages*, 1941; and *Little Gidding*, 1942. Like Eliot's other works, the *Four Quartets* does not yield easily to summary, but something of its nature may be gleaned from *East Coker*, which is concerned with progress towards faith. Section 4 is dominated by four significant images: the surgeon (= Christ), the nurse (= the Church), the hospital (= the World) and the millionaire (= Adam). Originally Adam had possessed paradise but had by his disobedience converted the world into a hospital:

> The whole earth is our hospital
> Endowed by the ruined millionaire,
> Wherein, if we do well, we shall
> Die of the absolute paternal care
> That will not leave us, but prevents us everywhere.

To rectify this situation Jesus Christ had entered the world, in which he is helped by the nurse:

> The wounded surgeon plies the steel
> That questions the distempered part;
> Beneath the bleeding hands we feel
> The sharp compassion of the healer's art
> Resolving the enigma of the fever chart.

> Our only health is the disease
> If we obey the dying nurse
> Whose constant care is not to please
> But to remind of our, and Adam's curse,
> And that, to be restored, our sickness must grow worse.

The means of healing is sacramental:

> The dripping blood our only drink,
> The bloody flesh our only food:
> In spite of which we like to think
> That we are sound, substantial flesh and blood—
> Again, in spite of that, we call this Friday good.

John Wain has written about the atmosphere of post-war Oxford. He entered the University in 1944, and was tutored by Lewis. Once each week he ascended the 'broad, shallow stairs' to the study in the 'new building' in Magdalen. In his autobiography, *Sprightly Running* (1962), Wain recalls the powerful impact of Lewis's dramatic personality: '... the thick-set body, the red face with its huge domed forehead, the dense clouds of smoke from a rapidly puffed cigarette or pipe, the brisk argumentative manner, and the love of debate which kept the conversation going at the race of some breathless game' (p. 138). Wain describes Lewis as 'militantly Christian' at a time when 'Christianity met with no real opposition among either the uneducated or the intelligentsia'. Indeed, 'Everybody to whom an imaginative and bookish youth naturally looked up, every figure which radiated intellectual glamour of any kind, was in the Christian camp' (p. 142). Other names linked with that of Lewis at this time were Coghill, Tolkien and Charles Williams. Wain recalls Lewis's attitude towards T. S. Eliot:

> The *Four Quartets* was on everyone's table – everyone, that is, who knew what the 'Spirit of the Age' was doing. And, whatever Eliot's views might once have been, the *Four Quartets* was a Christian – better still, an Anglican – masterpiece. Anglicanism, for years regarded as a quaint, intellectually dowdy set of attitudes (George Orwell called it 'the ecclesiastical equivalent of Trotskyism'), associated with the silver tea-pot on the vicarage lawn, suddenly became the adventurous spearhead of English intellectual and artistic life. So, at least, it looked from the point of view of an Oxford undergraduate in the mid-forties. Particularly if one happened to be studying literature; the interpretation of English poetry along Anglican lines was carried, in those years, to extraordinary lengths. The climax had been reached, a year or so before I arrived in Oxford, with Lewis's book on *Paradise Lost*, in which he achieved the feat of camouflaging Milton's Puritanism and making his epic look like a document of the purest Anglicanism. In the course of that book, Lewis had buried the hatchet with Eliot, whom he had attacked for years: 'I agree with him on matters of such importance that literary questions are by comparison trivial'. The Anglican ranks were closed at last. (p. 143)

By now the Imaginative Apologist had become, in Tolkien's laconic phrase, 'Everyman's theologian'.

Striking confirmation of Lewis's talent as an apologist for orthodox Christianity was given recently in an interview in *Eternity* (May 1984) by Rebecca Manley Pippert (whose job for Inter-Varsity Christian Fellowship is to train people in evangelism – her ideas are set forth in more detail in *Out of the Salt-Shaker*). When asked to name books that had had an early influence on her life she said this:

I was not raised a Christian. When I finally investigated Christianity, I went into our family's library, and decided I would try to find some book on it. There was just one. I remember taking it off the shelf and thinking, "Well, who's ever heard of some quack book called *Mere Christianity* by C. S. Lewis."

That was the turning point for me. I had thought Christianity wasn't worth investigating because there wasn't credibility. Then I found this relentlessly lucid mind that staggered me. There was also this tremendous integration of faith and reason. That was the book that really turned me around.

A different view is that of John Beversluis, a professor of philosphy at Butler University in America. In his book, *C. S. Lewis and the Search for Rational Religion* (Wm. B. Eerdmans, 1985), he cites Lewis's own statement: 'I am not asking anyone to accept Christianity if his best reasoning tells him that the weight of evidence is against it.' Beversluis accepts the implicit challenge. He believes that Lewis 'needs to be rescued not only from the evils of excessive hostility but also and equally from the evils of excessive loyalty. His apologetic writings deserve better than cavalier rejection or uncritical acceptance' (p. xiii). After closely examining Lewis's apologetic case, Beversluis brings in his verdict. 'His arguments for the existence of God fail. His answer to the problem of evil is unacceptable.... He is even guilty of trying to harmonise incompatible philosophical traditions. The failures accumulate, the inconsistencies remain, and the case for Christianity has not been made.'

In the final analysis, Beversluis suggests, Lewis is an outstanding example of steadfast personal commitment to orthodox Christianity but fails as a proponent of a traditional Christian apologetic.

Beversluis' decidedly iconoclastic volume will undoubtedly generate a good deal of discussion; it will also be an important tool – amongst many, it must be said – in the process of achieving a consensus concerning Lewis's case for Christianity. It ought to be read alongside Austen Farrer's close analysis of the Christian apologist's role in *Light on C. S. Lewis* (Bles, 1965), pp. 23–43, and also Michael Aeschliman's critique, *The Restitution of Man: C. S. Lewis and the Case Against Scientism*, which draws essentially different conclusions from those reached by Beversluis.[79]

CHAPTER FIVE

Science Fiction Too

The somewhat cryptic title of this chapter is intended simply to express admiration for Lewis's versatility in being able to turn his hand to writing science fiction in addition to his expertise in a large number of other fields. Science fiction is, of course, a highly specialised contemporary genre with precursors such as Jules Verne (who is commonly regarded as the founding father of science fiction) and H. G. Wells. The *Encyclopaedia Britannica* defines it as 'dealing with scientific discovery or development that, whether set in the future, in the fictitious present, or in the putative past, is superior to or simply other than that known to exist. Thus the word fiction in the term not only signifies, as in common usage, a work of the imagination but also applies directly to the word science. Depending upon the author's purpose, the degree to which the scientific element is fictionalised may range from a careful and informed extrapolation from known facts and principles to the most far-fetched and even flatly contradictory of speculations. What remains constant throughout is the appearance of plausibility, stemming from an at least surface allegiance to the attitudes, methods, and terminology of science.'[1]

This careful and comprehensive definition excludes works of fantasy which may offer or suggest explanations for great steps into the unknown in the form of scientific or pseudo-scientific hypotheses. Thus, Stoker's *Dracula* (1897) would not qualify, whereas R. L. Stevenson's *Strange Case of Dr Jekyll and Mr Hyde* (1886) would.

Lewis's total output in this field consists of three short stories, written near the end of his life, entitled 'The Shoddy Lands', 'Ministering Angels' and 'Forms of Things Unknown', and published in 1966 in *Of Other Worlds* and, more substantially, of his trilogy: *Out of the Silent Planet* (1938), *Voyage to Venus (Perelandra)* (1943), and *That Hideous Strength (1945)*. It is on these three major works that we shall concentrate. The method adopted will be to outline each story and to indicate the crucial aspects of these volumes in relation to each other and to Lewis's other published works; we shall also try to account for the continued success of this trilogy.

(1) *Out of the Silent Planet* (1938)[2]

First published in 1938 and re-printed many times subsequently, it was described by the 'Daily Telegraph' reviewer as 'striking and impressive'. The novelist L. P. Hartley judged it to be an 'original, interesting and well-written fantasy', while Sir Hugh Walpole considered it a 'very good book ... of thrilling interest as a story, but it is more than that: it is a kind of poem ... a unique thing'.

The chief character in this story – and the linking character between each of the three books – is Dr Ransom, a philologist and fellow of a Cambridge College. While on a walking tour, he encounters an old school and college acquaintance by the name of Devine whom he has always disliked. Devine's companion is Weston, massive and loud-mouthed, but a renowned physicist. Ransom's totally unexpected appearance was distinctly disturbing for the other two men because they had been ill-treating a local half-wit called Harry, a process interrupted by Ransom's arrival. The two men had intended using Harry for experimental purposes, but on discovering that Ransom's whereabouts had not been divulged to anybody, decided to use him instead. Consequently he was heavily drugged. Consciousness faded, and 'the last thing of which he was

aware was the grip of strong hands pulling him back into
the dark passage, and the sound of the closing door.'[3]
Ransom awoke to find himself looking at what he assumed
was the moon but was actually the Earth[4] (the silent planet
of the title.) Weston informed him that they were standing
'out from Earth about eighty-five thousand miles', and that
he was in transit to another planet called Malacandra (Mars).
Weston claimed to have been on a previous journey to
Malacandra, but refused to tell Ransom either the name of
the planet or how the ship in which they were travelling
worked. Athough troubled by the 'tyranny of heat and light'
within the spaceship, Ransom responded to the immense
delights of the heavens, the effect of contemplating their
huge and beautiful mystery being 'a progressive lightening
and exultation of heart'.

After a voyage lasting twenty-two days Ransom stepped
out of the spaceship. He first observed that the soil was pink
in colour, soft in texture, resembling india-rubber, and the
sky was pale blue. He soon discovered – before anything
else – how beautiful Malacandra was. Other discoveries
followed in rapid, often bewildering succession, including
the realisation that the creatures of Malacandra were capable
of speech and communication with each other. The next
stage in the story was learning to communicate with, and
experiencing a growing understanding of a gleaming
creature (a *hross** called Hyoi). Hyoi later took him on a boat
journey through a beautiful and fascinating landscape.
Living on Malacandra was an intoxicating experience for
Ransom, and during three weeks of discovery and delight
his understanding of the planet's culture was totally
transformed. He realised that the Malacandrians' culture
was far from primitive: they were acquainted with the
mysteries of astronomy, knew about Thulcandra (Earth),
dubbed by them 'the silent planet,' and were aware of the
Oyarsa who seemed to know everything.

The Oyarsa, he learned, lived in Meldilorn; they knew
everything and ruled everyone; had always been there; and
were not a *hross*, nor one of the *seroni*. He came to realise too

*For this and similar terms, see page 85.

that the Malacandrians were monogamous. They were also completely without knowledge of war. All of this caused Ransom to feel ashamed about Earth, a feeling accentuated by the fact that Malacandrians could be made miserable only by 'bent' creatures.

Two such 'bent' creatures, Weston and Devine, were responsible for the brutal killing of Hyoi. This caused Ransom to feel deep shame, so that he offered himself to Hyoi's fellows: 'I am in the hands of your people. ... they must do as they will ... but if they were wise they will kill me and certainly they will kill the other two.' He is told, however, that the 'One does not kill *hnau*'. Some days before this he had encountered a youthful she-*hross* speaking, as he had imagined, to herself. He was informed, however, that she had been speaking to an *eldil*, who are real, although invisible.

Ransom next confronts a *sorn* called Augray who informs him that Oyarsa is the greatest of the *eldila* who had been placed on Malacandra in order to rule over it. He discovered that the *eldil* was 'a thin, half-real body that can go through walls and rocks'. Then Augray showed him the earth, perhaps even England, though the tiredness of his eyes caused the picture to shake a little. Next morning Ransom awoke with a vague feeling that 'a great weight had been taken off his mind'. The pre-eminent consideration was put by him in the form of a question: 'And now how shall I find my way to Oyarsa?', to which Augray insisted that he should sit on his shoulder and thus begin his journey. Although seated eighteen feet in the air Ransom soon found that 'It was fun', not least because of the beautiful landscape that met this gaze, and he began to feel exhilarated.

The journey continued through numerous petrified forests and occasionally 'a long pallid face would show from a cavern mouth and exchange a horn-like greeting with the travellers, but for the most part the long valley, the rock-street of the silent people, was still and empty as the *harandra* itself'. Long before sundown they halted, at Augray's instruction, at the home of an older *sorn* (a scientist). The evening was spent in earnest and detailed conversation with the *seroni* asking Ransom a whole spate of questions.

Early next day Ransom took his allotted place on Augray's shoulder again and found himself ravished by the appearance before him of a new and wider *handramit*, below which lay an almost circular lake, in diameter twelve miles, in the middle of which was an island of 'pale red, smooth to the summit, and on the summit, a grove of such trees as man had never seen.'[16] He was then ferried across the lake by a *hross* who told him, in a hushed voice, that the 'island is all full of *eldila*'. He then went ashore to look at the island, but made the unnerving discovery that 'the surface of the island was subject to tiny variations of light and shade which no change in the sky accounted for'.[7]

His response to this phenomenon was a mixture of shyness, embarrassment and submission: an altogether uneasy sensation. Later he came across *pfifltriggi* drawing pictures of history and mythology, but a shock was in store for him, because when his eyes were drawn to a ball representing Earth, the ball was there, but 'where the flame-like figure should have been, a deep depression of irregular shape had been cut as if to erase it.'[8]

After a night spent in the richly decorated guesthouse he learned that Oyarsa had sent for him from Thulcandra (the 'silent planet' of the title – silent because 'the Oyarsa of your world ... became bent'). Another reason for sending for Ransom was that Oysarsa wished to know how Maleldil's war with the 'Bent One' had worked out.

Ransom's attempt to assuage Oyarsa's eager curiosity was interrupted by a procession carrying the dead bodies of *hrossa* on biers of some unknown metal. With them were Weston and Devine who were accused of their murder, and so were weaponless and vigilantly guarded by the armed *hrossa* about them. Typically, Devine advised Weston to say 'it was an accident'. Their whole attitude, far from being one of penitence, showed contempt for the people *they* assumed to be primitive – thus Weston brought out of his pocket a number of brightly coloured beads and proceeded to dangle them in front of the guards, muttering, 'Pretty, pretty. See, See.'[9] Even Devine realised that Weston was making a fool of himself. The dead *hrossa*, having been honoured by their fellows, were then made to disappear by a very strong wind.

The final stage of Ransom's adventures began with a long speech by Weston in which he said that he and Devine might be killed, but Oyarsa had little patience with either man, and it was decided that both should be sent back to Earth immediately; Oyarsa was unimpressed by the protestations of the hapless pair, wishing only to talk to Ransom and to determine the future. Ransom, given the option of remaining in Malacandra or of attempting the hazardous journey back to Earth, chose to return.

Thus far we have considered only the outlines of the story, and certain terms have been used with little or no explanation, so it might be useful to list some of them now:

Eldil, (eldila or eldils)	– invisible beings
Handramit	– the lowland
Harandra	– the highland
Hman	– man
Hnakra	– evil monster
Hnau	– rational beings
Hross (hrossa) }	the three rational
Pfiltrig (pfiltriggi) }	– species (of *hnau*)
Sorn (seroni) }	inhabiting Malcandra
Malacandra	– the old planet (Mars)
Meldilorn	– the sacred island
Maleldil-the-young	– creator and ruler
Oyarsa	– the great eldil
Thulcandra	– the silent world.

While the reason why Lewis wrote *Out of the Silent Planet* is largely a matter of conjecture,[10] there is considerable agreement that it is a highly imaginative work, blending intention and fact to give credibility to the incredible. Lewis's ability to describe scenes in it is both powerful and evocative, affording the reader the same sort of intensity and pleasure as in the science fiction of, say, Ray Bradbury.

The characterisation too is vigorous and subtle. Weston and Devine are repulsive, not least because of their cold unconcern for anybody or anything else. From the very beginning of the book we feel their callous disregard for other people. They lie, coerce, bully, contrive and use violence to achieve their own particular diabolical ends, and as the story unfolds we begin to share Ransom's feelings of disgust, culminating in the murders towards the end of the book. Weston compounds his crime in Ransom's eyes by speaking patronisingly to space creatures, but succeeds only in making himself look ridiculous. Nor do we have any sympathy when judgement is pronounced upon them; they deserve to be returned to Earth. Ransom, on the other hand, is a gentler figure, not only academic but an earthy person who on his return walked into a village pub with a request for a pint of beer.

Emphasis must be placed on the didactic and theological elements in the book, an approach sanctioned by Lewis in a letter dated 9th July 1939:

> You will be both grieved and amused to hear that out of about 60 reviews only 2 showed any knowledge that my idea of the fall of the Bent One was anything but an invention of my own. But if there only was someone with a richer talent and more leisure I think that his greater ignorance might be a help to the evangelisation of England; any amount of theology can now be smuggled into people's minds under cover of romance without their knowing it.[11]

The high value he placed on reason is as apparent in this work as it is in *The Pilgrim's Regress*. For example, Ransom discovered to his great amazement that at least three species have the power of rational thought on Malacandra without destroying each other. Again, the intense reality of death is given full expression.

But the most crucial issue concerns the way in which we are meant to interpret this story. Obviously it can stand on its own, as an unit, a complete science fiction story. Equally clearly it can be read as part of the trilogy of stories he wrote with the character of Ransom linking the three. Another plausible approach is to view it in satirical terms, by which Lewis allows his characters to make comments on and criticisms about the inhabitants of Earth from the vantage point of space, in a manner reminiscent of Swift, for example, in *Gulliver's Travels*. All of these suggestions have something to commend them, nor is there any need to adopt an exclusive posture. Ultimately *Out of the Silent Planet* must be assessed by literary standards, in terms of its imaginative quality and its power to convince us about the life and inhabitants of Mars. In my judgment it does this as surely as Wells convinces us about the reality and awesomeness of the invasion of Earth by the Martians in *War of the Worlds*. Add to this its intellectual coherence and its reflection of Christian standards, and the picture emerges of an extremely impressive and wide-ranging book, though not, I think, the best of his trilogy. The Christian elements were valued by some readers and antagonised others, while a third group failed to appreciate these facets of the book; not that this matters in itself. The reception accorded *Out of the Silent Planet* was on the whole favourable, but it did not begin to sell spectacularly until *The Screwtape Letters* were published in 1942, placing C. S. Lewis onto a world-wide stage.

(2) *Voyage to Venus [Perelandra]* (1943)

Writing to Arthur Greeves on 23rd December 1941, Lewis said that he was working on a sequel to *Out of the Silent Planet* in which the same man journeys to Venus. He defined the central idea of the volume as follows:

> Venus is at the Adam-and-Eve stage: i.e. the first two rational creatures have just appeared and are still innocent. My hero arrives in time to prevent their 'falling' as the first pair did.[12]

Earlier, in a letter to Sister Penelope, he laid down some of the difficulties involved in such a project; in particular the fact that the Eve of Venus has to combine the mutually contradictory elements found in the Blessed Virgin and a Pagan Goddess.[12] The work was eventually published in 1943, and in a brief prefatory note Lewis said that *Perelandra* could be read by itself or as a sequel to *Out of the Silent Planet*; further that all the human characters in the book are entirely fictitious, none of them being allegorical. Historically it was probably his work on *Paradise Lost* between 1939 and 1941 which gave Lewis the essential ideas for *Perelandra*, but as far as the precise origin is concerned, there is – as with *Out of the Silent Planet* – only conjecture.[13]

The work opens with a narrator (later identified as Lewis himself), and Dr Ransom, whose function links this volume and the earlier one. Following an eerie uncomfortable journey and arrival at Ransom's cottage the narrator and Ransom met. The most noticeable thing in the room was a big white object which was a 'coffin-shaped casket', and open. Not a space-ship in the usual sense of the word, it was intended for Ransom's journey, not to Malacandra, but to Perelandra (that is, Venus). This journey was considered to be necessary because 'The black archon – our own bent Oyarsa – is meditating some sort of attack on Perelandra' and it was being undertaken on orders, not from Oyarsa, but from 'much higher up.' Ransom was humble and self-effacing about being chosen for such a great project.

He was rather vague about the precise duration of the journey, but, in fact, he was away for a whole year, after which he told his story as narrated below.

On approaching Mars, Ransom was shocked to realise that, in fact, the casket was 'melting, dissolving away, giving place to an indescribable confusion of colour – a rich, varied world in which nothing, for the moment, seemed palpable'. His first impressions were of something slanted, after which he found himself being transported on gigantic waves in a land of variegated and luscious colours: emeralds, silver, greens, etc.

His initial feelings were those of ecstatic, indeed excessive joy, . . . 'Ransom himself could only describe it by saying that for his first few days on Perelandra he was haunted, not by a feeling of guilt, but by surprise that he had no such feeling'. He found walking extremely difficult; in fact, he had to spend several hours teaching himself to walk. Eventually he reached the 'wooded part' with its exotic fruit which was like the discovery' of a totally new *genus* of pleasures, something unheard of among men, out of all reckoning, beyond all covenant. For one draught of this on Earth wars would be fought and nations betrayed. It could not be classified. He could never tell us, when he came back from the world of men, whether it was sharp or sweet, savoury or voluptuous, creamy or piercing.' Such was the enjoyment, that Ransom felt as if he had been conveyed to an 'uninhabitable world, and the terror added, as it were, a razor-edge to all that profusion of pleasure'. An 'absolute blackness' then took over and sleep came 'like a fruit which falls into the hand almost before you have touched the stem'.

Next day he encountered a 'small dragon covered with scales of red-gold'. At first Ransom wondered whether the animal was dangerous, but suddenly it turned away from him and began to tear up the herbage with 'great avidity'. After a meal Ransom went down to the water's edge to drink, but before he arrived there it was already 'up to the water's edge. The island at that moment was a little valley of bright land nestling between hills of green water, and as he lay on his belly to drink he had the extraordinary experience of dipping his mouth in a sea that was higher than the shore.' Then he saw in the distance a creature that looked like a man, but he realised that the green man was not a man at all, but a woman, who stood up amidst beasts and birds of various shapes and hues. The Green Lady beckoned the animals to behold Ransom. She possessed a calmness quite unknown to inhabitants of Earth and he realised that Venus was at a stage before the fall of Man; unfallen humanity no less, 'a calm which no storm had ever preceded'.[14] Ransom spoke to her in the Malacandrian language, but tantalisingly, just as he was about to speak to her again, a wave rose between them and took her out of his sight. In response to this he flung himself into the water and eventually found himself safe but out of breath on the dry, 'sweet-scented, undulating surface' of the island. At his next meeting with the Green Lady he discovered how different she was from earth dwellers. She did not possess their self-consciousness or, more importantly, their knowledge of evil. She had an enchantingly child-like quality about her. Nor did she know the meaning of the word 'rubbish'. Eventually Ransom fell back, into a 'dreamless sleep', after which he was led back to her by a dragon, and their conversation resumed, during which he discovered that only the Lady and the King actually inhabited the planet.

She had not encountered death, but she viewed freedom as something that existed as an entity in and of itself. Thus was introduced into her mind the possibility of going against Madeldil's will. The result of all this was that the Lady began to look at him with a 'new and more judicial expression'. In essence, what had happened was that both the Lady and Ransom had started on a journey of *self-discovery*. With much to ponder over she withdrew and Ransom re-traced his steps through the deep vegetation until they were out of each other's sight.

As Ransom continued his journey around the island he discovered that although it had a base of rough country, the valleys had a hint of vegetation, and that some of it was inhabitable land. After surveying the beautiful plateau, he was approached by Weston whose 'massive egoism' impaired Ransom's blissful mood, and he was further disconcerted when Weston brandished a revolver. Weston, much to Ransom's amazement, claimed to be searching for the same things as Ransom: 'the spread of spirituality'. To achieve this end Weston would not allow anything to stand in his way; he would ruthlessly cheat, lie, even murder to get his own way. The conversation ended frighteningly when Weston suffered various convulsions. The stroke or epileptic fit did, however, decrease in intensity, after which Ransom, feeling angry, lonely, and frustrated lapsed into a disturbed sleep.

Next day, after ascending to the central plateau, Ransom was transported on the back of a great silvery fish to the floating islands. Subsequently he spoke with Weston, who revealed that he was trying to tempt the Lady firstly to go against Maleldil's wishes not to dwell on the Fixed Land, and secondly to view herself as a heroic figure. His approach was not at all bullying or abrupt, rather it was quietly persistent and patient. Once again sleep intervened. By now a clear and definite pattern had emerged, involving Weston's plodding, unyielding temptation of the Lady, all his arguments being calculated to motivate her to transgress the King's edicts and commands. His chief weapon, in all of this, was to play on what has been commonly called 'female vanity'.

Ransom, however, though racked by agonies of conscience and internal doubts, realised that the fate of Venus lay not in the hands of the enemy but in God's and he understood that faith needed to be exercised; all that was required was the will and the resolve to oppose the enemy, a realisation which gave him immense joy. Along with this was the awareness that Ransom had the means whereby Perelandra would be saved from the Fall. Foretastes of future splendour were given to him, but Ransom decided to return to Earth.

Critics of weight and substance consider *Perelandra* to be one of Lewis's finest imaginative works,[15] rivalled only by *Till We Have Faces*, Lightness of touch, imaginative ingenuity and descriptive felicity all combine in a work that stands better as an independent unit than do the two other parts of the trilogy. Temptation is the dominating theme of *Perelandra*. A world of utter bliss is invaded by earth visitors, one of whom, at least, comes with evil intentions. A planet without sin, without jealousy, without the competitive urge of success, sees the arrival of Weston, a man prepared to manipulate, persuade, coerce and lie; in short to adopt any expedient stratagem to achieve his particular ends, which are to pervert the idyllic world in which Maleldil and his creatures exist happily, bound together by an attitude of trust and cooperation. The intensity of the struggle – truly an epic one – is portrayed forcefully in chapters 10 and 11; for example where Ransom realised that Weston's arguments to the Lady were characterised by one quality above all others: 'It regarded intelligence simply and solely as a weapon ... a device necessary to certain ends ... it assumed reason as externally and inorganically as it had assumed Weston's body.' As with Eve in Paradise Lost (Book 9), the Lady's sense of adventure and vanity is appealed to, her tendency to self-dramatisation: 'a self-admiring inclination to seize the grand rôle in the drama of the world'. Temptations, then, to 'fatuous pride, to megalomania' are seen by Ransom to be part of a spiritual struggle, a herculean contest with a diabolic force. Weston's totally perverted reasoning is the result of a will that has been taken over by an alien force. In cosmic terms, he has chosen to do what is forbidden by God.

This Dark Power in the universe is described by Lewis in *Mere Christianity* as 'the fatal flaw' which always 'brings the selfish and cruel people to the top and it all slides back into misery and ruin'. *Perelandra* is a powerful vehicle for Lewis's theological speculations and exposition, not just on the theme of obedience and disobedience and its relationship to the idea of Redemption, but on a large number of related issues, including the idea of God as 'the centre of the universe', Christ's love and substitutionary sacrifice, and his notions about hell.

Inevitably too in *Perelandra* we observe his insistence on the importance of myth:

> Ransom had been perceiving that the triple distinction of truth from myth and of both from fact was purely terrestrial – was part and parcel of that unhappy division between soul and body which resulted from the Fall. Even on earth the sacraments existed as a permanent reminder that the division was neither wholesome nor final. The Incarnation had been the beginning of its disappearance.[16]

Much of what Lewis says in this book, therefore, relates to his scale of values in general. *Perelandra* also embodies Lewis's forebodings about the whole question of inter-planetary travel and Weston's brand of science which would be prepared to wipe out the inhabitants of other planets in order to preserve alive the human race, whatever the cost in terms of suffering for the dwellers on those planets.

This volume is fascinating because of its portrayal of the immense and unremitting battle between good and evil which drew out all Lewis's imaginative abilities. It is all the more attactive because its language has a poetic quality which, in my opinion, surpasses anything found in the other two novels.

(3) *That Hideous Strength* (1945)

Before coming to the main lines of the story it is pertinent to recall Lewis's own preface to this work:

This is a 'tall story' about devilry, though it has behind it a serious 'point' which I have tried to make in my *Abolition of Man*. In the story the outer rim of that devilry had to be shown touching the life of some ordinary and respectable profession. I selected my own profession, not, of course, because I think Fellows of Colleges more likely to be thus corrupted than anyone else, but because my own profession is naturally that which I know best. A very small university is imagined because that has certain conveniences for fiction. Edgestow has no resemblance, save for its smallness, to Durham – a university with which the only connection I have ever had was entirely pleasant.[17]

The vivid opening scene of the book is both domestic and ordinary. Jane Studdock was disenchanted, bored and bitter with life. Frustrated with the restrictions of marriage, she still hoped to complete her doctoral thesis on the poet John Donne, but a recurring dream[18] interrupted all attempts at productive work. Her husband, Mark, a sociologist, had been a fellow at Bracton College in the university town of Edgestow for five years. Highly intelligent, and confident of his own ability, he delighted to be considered a part of the progressive element in the college. A proud, sensitive man, he did not like to be reminded that he had once been not only outside the progressive element but also outside the college itself.

The college surroundings were dominated by Bragdon Wood, a secluded and revered area, which the college was now contemplating selling to the National Institute of Coordinated Experiments (N.I.C.E.), formerly located at Oxford, Cambridge, and London. Largely free from the restraints of economy, it was 'the first-fruit of that constructive fusion between the state and the laboratory on which so many thoughtful people base their hopes of a better world'. The N.I.C.E.'s coming to Edgestow was dependent on gaining Bragdon Wood as a site for its work. The progressives in the college manage to defeat the so-called 'Diehards', and to ensure the sale of the Wood. A significant Arthurian interest affected the site, since Merlin, a fifth-century Christian druid, was reputedly buried under Bragdon Wood without, in fact, being dead.

The reason for N.I.C.E.'s coming to Bracton is brought out
by Lord Feverstone at a dinner party in the house of the
Warden, Charles Place. Their intention was 'sterilisation of
the unfit, liquidation of backward races, selective breeding.
Then real education, including pre-natal education.' Mark
was gradually drawn into the N.I.C.E. circle (by Feverstone),
though not as yet as a member of the magical 'inner cicle'. At
one meeting of the N.I.C.E. Mark encountered Hengist ('Bill
the Blizzard' to the progessive members of the college) who
assured him that the organisation would inevitably acquire
the wood because 'they had powers to compel a sale'.
Meanwhile Jane who was becoming attached to a group in a
neighbouring village, presided over by Ransom, was told
that her dreams (referred to at the beginning of this chapter)
consisted of 'real things' that they were partly true, and that
they fitted in with information already in the possession of
the group. She was invited to join them, and thus became
committed to opposing the N.I.C.E. Chaos followed the
arrival of the N.I.C.E. in Edgestow, with lorries, traction
engines and other raucous machinery, besides other perils
which were more personal and frightening.

Within the ambit of the N.I.C.E. moved the curious figure
of 'the Reverend Straik', who realised that this programme
would inevitably be resisted, perhaps violently so. The
cloistered calm of Bracton College, too, was shattered in a
frightening way, and such disturbances naturally led to
conflicting loyalties, so that Mark had to decide where his
allegiance lay. When confronted by Mrs Hardcastle, the
implacable Captain of the Women's Auxiliary Institutional
Police, he requested a place in the 'Sociological Department'.
Subsequently, a clear indication of the changing situation
was the fact that Jane was savagely tortured, her body being
burned with cigars.

Two forces were now in competition, and, realising that
ultimate victory would depend on Merlin's supernatural
powers, each faction became anxious to recover the body
hidden in the recesses of Bragdon Wood. Mark was allowed
to meet the 'Head' of N.I.C.E. This was in fact the guillotined
head of Alcasan, a criminal, which had been scientifically
preserved by N.I.C.E. who intended using it to immortalise

man, thus making him independent of nature. In truth this head was nothing less than Earth's malign *eldila*, who controlled the leaders and Head at Belbury. Ransom was certain that Merlin also would join the Belbury organisation if the N.I.C.E. reached him first.

It was vital to ascertain the exact place of Merlin's departure from an underground burial chamber located in the wood. The search proved abortive, since Merlin had himself left the grave in order to ally himself with Ransom and his party. Having spoken with them, he went to Belbury, where he was welcome and shown the mysteries of the N.I.C.E., including that of the guillotined head. His arrival at Belbury was heralded by a banquet which, at first, resembled that of any other banquet. The speakers became confused by Merlin's magical powers, and began to speak gibberish. Confusion was followed by terror and eventually the place was set alight. All the inhabitants of Edgestow find themselves impelled to leave it – to escape the destruction which mysteriously overwhelms it. The relationship between Mark and Jane is transformed. He finds thoughts of unforgettable failure rising in his imagination; but he recognised his own 'clumsy importunity' and his unworthy motives. The novel ends on a note of love, mutual acceptance and humility, after a sequence of horrifying events and even more horrifying people.

That Hideous Strength is lengthy and often tortuous. Lewis said it 'was unanimously damned by the reviewers'. Others, like Roger Lancelyn Green, were enraptured by it, while Dorothy Sayers felt it was 'tremendously full of good things – perhaps almost too full'. Its main theme – that of a group of scientists intent on taking over the world – needs to be read in the light of the concern that underlies *The Abolition of Man* (first published in 1938), in which Lewis turned his attention to the question of objective and subjective values. Adherence to objective values tended to promote responsible attitudes; but people are increasingly conditioned by an assertive propaganda based on continually shifting concepts. He feared the triumph of an all powerful scientific attitude which would require the conditioning of the whole of human life and existence:

The real picutre is that of one dominant age – let us suppose the hundredth century AD – which resists all previous ages most successfully and dominates all subsequent ages most irresistibly, and thus is the real master of the human species. But then within this master generation (itself an infinitesimal minority of the species) the power will be exercised by a minority smaller still. Man's conquest of Nature, if the dreams of some scientific planners are realized, means the rule of a few hundreds of men over billions upon billions of men. There neither is nor can be any simple increase of power on Man's side. Each new power won *by* man is a power *over* man as well. Each advance leaves him weaker as well as stronger. In every victory, besides being the general who triumphs, he is also the prisoner who follows the triumphal car.[19]

Such men would not accept a doctrine of objective validity and would recognise only *their* system of values. This postulate sums up the thinking behind much of *That Hideous Strength*: world domination is desired by unscrupulous men; the same terrifying wish for ultimate power which animated Weston in *Perelandra*. My personal feeling is that, for several reasons, this work is the least satisfactory of the trilogy. One is undoubtedly its length. It would have been far better if Lewis had tailored the material to form two books instead of its present bulky form. Its Arthurian elements too are likely to be unknown to a large number of readers who have no interest in this rather specialised literary field. They are complex, remote and unfamiliar to most people. On the other hand, it could be claimed that the plot is richly imaginative. The parts which portray Bracton College at work, with all its petty jealousies, rivalries and personality clashes, are skilful and effective; it is not inappropriate to compare these sections with C. P. Snow's masterly exposé of *The Masters*. Certainly Lewis's characters are varied, diverse, and portrayed with perception and insight. It is a vast work, containing within itself a number of disparate elements, and experience shows that it yields its pearls grudgingly and only after care is taken in reading and re-reading it.

It is not easy to assess Lewis's work within the field of science fiction. Nowadays the term covers an almost infinite variety of material. Tentatively, the *genre* may be said to include some of the following components:

(1) *An Unknown World or Civilisation*

Science Fiction has to do with things that do not exist as yet (as far as we know), or perhaps with the world as it may be in the future. It does not reflect (as the novel does) the world as we know it, or as it existed during an author's life-time, as for example, Dickens's works reflect the social world and conditions in the nineteenth-century.

(2) *Conflict*

As Harvey Hallsmith says in *Space on the Bookshelf*,[20] 'All of Science Fiction is a battlefield. Conflict, physical or mental, dominates the pages of Science Fiction.' It can be the sort of physical menace posed by the monster of immense proportions in Ray Bradbury's *The Sound of Thunder*; or it may deal with the deliberate prevention of the spread of ideas as in *Fahrenheit 451* (Bradbury again); or it may be political, as in *1984*, Orwell's chillingly disturbing and depressing classic, which envisages a totalitarian society presided over by a ruthless dictator euphemistically described as 'Big Brother'. *1984* is not only a satire but also an extremely moving story of Winston Smith's unavailing fight against technology.

(3) *Brilliant Imagination*

Under this heading we may include such matters as the evocation of character, the story line, and certainly descriptive power. (There is no better example than Bradbury's well-known description of the Mechanical Hound in *Fahrenheit 451*, where the author does not attempt a comprehensive or systematic picture of the beast. He supplies a few crucial details, creates a feeling of mindless menace, and allows our imaginations to do the rest.)

(4) *Alien Invaders*

A prominent aspect of Science Fiction is the threat to Earth from alien invaders. Possibly the most famous example is

The War of the Worlds (H. G. Wells), a story about the Martians' invasion of Earth. The appearance of the first Martian is described factually, and is infinitely more powerful in its effect than anything that could be produced through emotional exaggeration. Many writers have followed Wells, among them John Wyndham who, in *The Day of the Triffids*, portrays the invasion of a part of South-East England by the Triffids who resemble gigantic mobile vegetables and whose predilections are for killing people and eating putrefying human flesh.

(5) *Space Travel*

Science Fiction from the very start has been linked with the idea of space travel. Notable examples are *Deathworld*, by Harry Harrison, in which the setting for the study is Pyrrus, a small planet where all forms of life are hostile to human beings, and *The Impossible Star*, by Brian Aldiss.

(6) *Concern with Vital Issues*

Not all Science Fiction is trivially escapist: 'In fact, most science fiction is concerned, implicitly if not explicitly, with really important issues. It's continually asking basic questions – what is our true identity, what sort of nature do we have, are we the sole lords of creation, do we, as a species, deserve to survive? Any science fiction reader will at least have acquired a few healthy doubts about the natural superiority of mankind' (Harvey Hallsmith). Arthur Clarke's work is especially relevant in this context with *Childhood's End* and *Nine Billion Names of God*.

All these characteristic features of Science Fiction are discernible in Lewis's trilogy; he belongs to the mainstream of this genre. The invaders, it is true, move in space *from* earth *to* the planets, but this is only a minor difference. To all of this must be added his allegorical intention, an aspect recognised by J. A. W. Bennett in the *Dictionary of National Biography 1961–1970*, article on C. S. Lewis, and by Kingsley Amis, in *New Maps of Hell* (New English Library, 1961). Amis comments: 'Religion in the straightforward sense is treated thematically in the fantasy novels of C. S. Lewis and of Charles Williams.'

What is the current view of Lewis's status as a writer of science fiction? For an answer we can appeal to *The Encyclopedia of Science Fiction*, edited by Peter Nicholls (Granada, 1981). It has this to say about *Out of the Silent Planet* and *Voyage to Venus*: 'The first two novels are interplanetary romances, with strong traces of medieval mythology; each planet is seen as having a tutelary spirit; those of the other planets are both good and accessible; that of Earth is fallen, twisted and not known directly by most humans. These two books are powerfully imagined, although their scientific content is intermittently absurd; the effect of lesser gravity on Martian plant and animal life is rendered with great economy and vividness, as is Ransom's first perception of the water world of Venus, a rich exercise in PERCEPTION. ... The religious allegory of *Perelandra*, however, in which an evil scientist plays Satanic tempter to the female ruler of Venus, a new Eve, is deeply conservative, and also sexist, in its courtly, romantic (and some may think dehumanizing) view of womanhood.' It views *That Hideous Strength* as being 'more directly occult in its genre machinery than either of its predecessors. The fury of CSL's attack on scientific II "humanism" (science directed towards purely worldly ends) is very nearly unbalanced, and leads to a grossly melodramatic caricature of scientists and their government-supported research units in general, and against H. G. Wells in particular, here grotesquely envisaged as a vulgar cockney journalist, Jules.' Its final conclusion is that 'this trilogy is, for all its propagandizing, in comparison to most genres, a richly imagined work, and has attained classic status'.

CHAPTER SIX

Letter Writer Extraordinary

Lewis's influence spread far beyond the confines of Oxford and Cambridge Universities where he spent the whole of his professional and working life. There were many reasons for this. In the first place there was the effect of his teaching and lecturing. Secondly, there was the publication of his scholarly works, articles, reviews, sermons, religious volumes, science fiction, and of the Narnia Chronicles. A third factor, though not so widely appreciated, was his vast correspondence with adults – of all ages, temperaments, cultures, religions and backgrounds – and children throughout the world. Letters addressed to him arrived relentlessly at Magdalen, Magdalene, and 'The Kilns', and were all dealt with as soon as he possibly could, his replies being written in his own handwriting. Since his death on 22nd November 1963 in Oxford, three volumes of his letters have been published: (1) *Letters of C. S. Lewis*, edited by W. H. Lewis (1966); (2) *Letters To An American Lady*, edited by Clyde S. Kilby (1969); (3) *They Stand Together: The Letters of C. S. Lewis to Arthur Greeves 1914–63*, edited by Walter Hooper (1979)

The first of these volumes, edited by his brother, Warren Lewis, is only a selection of the 'Lewis Papers' which consist of over 3500 pages of letters, diaries and other family documents. Warren spent a great deal of time in his retirement going through these family papers, and classifying them. In his 'Memoir' at the beginning of the book he explains why only a 'selection' was made for publication: 'Not all the letters that Jack wrote were of permanent and public interest; he sometimes repeated himself; and a few letters, or parts of letters, must be held back on grounds of charity or discretion. In certain cases, the names of correspondents have been altered or suppressed, for sufficient reason.'

The second volume contains more than a hundred letters written between 26th October 1950 and 30th August 1963 (within three months of his death). They were written to a woman who died in 1978. These letters are as good an indication as any of his almost saintly willingness to answer even the most trivial of enquiries. Some of the letters are very brief indeed, or as he put it, 'just a scrape of the pen', and it is apparent that this lady wrote to him with great (some would say obsessive) regularity and without any real appreciation of the demands on his time. Her letters followed him everywhere, even on holiday, as one of his replies headed 'Somewhere in Eire' (dated 18th August 1956) shows:

Dear Mary

It's no good giving you an address for I am moving about. Your letter of Aug. 12th reached me today. I am delighted to hear about the job. It sounds exactly the thing, sent by God, at your most need. I will never laugh at anyone for grieving over a loved beast. I think God wants us to love Him *more*, not to love creatures (even animals) *less*. We love everything *in one way* too much (i.e. at the expense of our love for Him) but in another way we love everything too little.

No person, animal, flower, or even pebble, has ever been loved too much — i.e. more than every one of God's works deserves. But you need not feel "like a murderer". Rather rejoice that God's law allows you to extend to Fanda that last mercy which (no doubt, quite rightly) we are forbidden to extend to suffering humans. You'll get over this. ...

I'm writing on a dressing table in a small, dark hotel bedroom, very sleepy, so I'll close. God bless you — and Fanda!

Yours

Jack Lewis[2]

The third volume, majestically edited by Walter Hooper, consists of a correspondence which spanned a period of fifty years: the first letter is dated June 1914, the last 11th September 1963. Part of it reads poignantly:

> 'The only real snag is that it looks as if you and I shall never meet again in this life. This often saddens me v. much ... I am glad you are fairly well and have a housekeeper. But oh Arthur, never to see you again.'[3]

Lewis and Arthur Greeves had been life-long friends, and yet were different in almost every way. Lewis was, by any reckoning, an intellectual 'giant' with three 'Firsts' to his credit, whereas Greeves had studied Art at the Slade and in Paris without achieving any sort of excellence. Lewis had lived a full and often exhausting life at Oxford and Cambridge, while Greeves had lived quietly on a private income in Ireland and had done little else. Lewis was a 'larger than life' character, combative, famous and brilliant, whereas Greeves was shy, modest, remaining an essentially 'shadowy' figure.

What then drew them together? The answer, undoubtedly, is their shared passion for literature, their love of myth, and their search for Joy. As Lewis says in a letter dated 6th June 1916: 'You are a very good judge for me because our tastes run in the same direction.'[4] Clearly, too, Lewis valued Greeves's literary judgement and often sent him manuscripts for appraisal and proof-reading; nor was Greeves reluctant in turn to make constructive criticisms of what he read. He made, for example, a number of observations on the style and content of *The Pilgrim's Regress* before its publication, which Lewis took seriously and to which he replied at considerable length. Greeves was a sort of confidant or 'father-confessor' for Lewis, and their friendship was rewarding for both of them: they needed each other. Lewis could confide in Greeves, and he did so about his relationship with Joy Davidman:

> 'The other affair remains where it did. I don't feel the point about a false position. Everyone whom it concerned wd. be told.

The reality wd. be from my point of view, adultery and therefore mustn't happen (An easy resolution when one doesn't in the least want it).'[5]

There are various references, too, to Warren Lewis's drinking problem:

'After 9 months of perfect tee-totalism (we flattered ourselves it was a real cure) W. has started drinking again and the elaborate joint holidays we had planned for us in the summer will probably have to be cancelled.'[6]

Taken together, these volumes of Lewis's letters preserve and re-animate the main events of his life from 1914 right through to within a month of his death: his intense dislike of Malvern College; his great delight in life under Kirkpatrick at Great Bookham; his entry into University College, Oxford, and his brilliant undergraduate career there; his often difficult relationship with his father, and his more amiable companionship with his brother; academic routine at Magdalen and Magdalene; the domestic complexities of life with Mrs Moore; his deserved elevation to a professorial chair at Cambridge after a series of disappointments at Oxford; his bitter-sweet relationship with Joy Davidman; her death from cancer in 1960; his growing ill-health, culminating in his resignation from the Chair of Medieval and Renaissance English at Cambridge where he had been extremely happy and contented; the final few months when and he and his brother were together again, the wheel having come full circle.

The letters are fascinating for the many glimpses they give us of Lewis 'the man' and Lewis 'the scholar'. They contain clear evidence that he was prepared to advise his pupils in a quite specific and detailed way as the following letter, dated 18th June 1931, shows:

Now as to work. If you are staying up over the week-end and could call on me on Saturday morning we could discuss this. If this is impossible, my present advice is this:—
Doing Chaucer and Shakespeare in the same term seems to me a hazardous experiment, unless there is some special reason

which I don't know yet. Our usual plan here is to spend a term
on Chaucer and his contemporaries. As regards reading for the
Vac., my general view is that the Vac. should be given chiefly to
reading the actual literary texts, without much attention to
problems, getting thoroughly familiar with stories, situation,
and style, and so having all the data for *aesthetic* judgement
ready; then the term can be kept for more scholarly reading.
Thus, if you were doing Chaucer and contemporaries next term,
I shd. advise you to read Chaucer himself, Langland (if you can
get Skeat's edtn., the selection is not much good), Gower (again
Macaulay's big edtn. if possible, not so that you may read every
word of the *Confessio* but so that you may select yourself—not
forgetting the end which is one of the best bits), Gawain
(Tolkien and Gordon's edtn.) Sisam's XIV century prose and
verse (all the pieces of any literary significance). If you can
borrow Ritson's *Metrical Romance* so much the better.

But perhaps you have read all these before. If so, and if there
are other special circumstances, we must try to meet. If Saturday
is impossible, ring me up on Friday and I will squeeze in a time
somehow or other.[7]

They illustrate, too, one of his life-long emphases, namely
that literary texts are to be read *first hand*, and that aesthetic
and other judgements are to be made on a solid bedrock of
knowledge. Not for him second-hand acquaintance with
literary works such as can be gained from reading the views
of the critics instead of the original. He had little time for or
patience with students who offered him someone else's
work as their own. On one occasion he detected a pupil
doing this: 'I told him I was not a detective nor even a
schoolmaster, nor a nurse, and that I absolutely refused to
take any precaution against this puerile trick: that I'd soon
as think it my business to see that he washed behind his
ears or wiped his bottom.'[8] The upshot of this incident was
that the unfortunate student left the university the next
week and Lewis never saw him again. What staggered
Lewis was that any man could prefer 'the galley-slave labour
of transcription to the freeman work of attempting an essay
on his own'.[9] Lewis was, of course, right in his attitude, but
his utterly forthright response leaves one with a sneaking
sympathy for the undergraduate exposing his puny knowledge to a man of Lewis's intellectual stature.

Although he was noted for his determinedly impersonal reactions to his students, and for regarding tutorial work as a burdensome activity, yet his letters show that he was capable of extreme kindness towards his pupils, especially if he felt they deserved encouragement and advice. Those with experience of university tutors may well feel that the undergraduates who were given such careful direction by Lewis were fortunate indeed.[10]

He responded wholeheartedly to enquiries from children; he never spoke down to them, as a lesser man might have done. Here he is giving an American schoolgirl general guidance on writing:

(1) Turn off the Radio.

(2) Read all the good books you can, and avoid nearly all magazines.

(3) Always write (and read) with the ear, not the eye. You shd. hear every sentence you write as if it was being read aloud or spoken. If it does not sound nice, try again.

(4) Write about what really interests you, whether it is real things or imaginary things, and nothing else. (Notice this means that if you are interested *only* in writing you will never be a writer, because you will have nothing to write about. ...)

(5) Take great pains to be *clear*. Remember that though you start by knowing what you mean, the reader doesn't, and a single ill-chosen word may lead him to a total misunderstanding. In a story it is terribly easy just to forget that you have not told the reader something that he wants to know— the whole picture is so clear in your own mind that you forget that it isn't the same in his.

(6) When you give up a bit of work don't (unless it is hopelessly bad) throw it away. Put it in a drawer. It may come in useful later. Much of my best work, or what I think my best, is the re-writing of things begun and abandoned years earlier.

(7) Don't use a typewriter. The noise will destroy your sense of rhythm, which still needs years of training.

(8) Be sure you know the meaning (or meanings) of every word you use.[11]

Two aspects of this letters are worth noting for they apply to much of Lewis's own writing: the insistence on having something of value to say, on the one hand, and the desirability of clarity, on the other hand.

He also wrote many letters giving advice of a general or personal nature. Humanity, common sense, honesty all shine through his letters; they reveal him as a courteous person who would, for example, take the trouble to explain at some length why he had left a lady's letter unanswered:

> I am extremely sorry (and at such a time too) to have left your letter of April 14th so long unanswered. But there was a chapter of obstacles. First, you put no address on the letter and the outside of the envelope had got damp so the the address was illegible. Second, I was in Cambridge (where your letter was forwarded) and your address in the files here. Thirdly, my brother was away ill, so that I couldn't send mine to him to be addressed. Fourthly, there was a railway strike which prevented me coming home last week-end as I would normally have done. That brings us to yesterday![13]

The lady in question wrote frequently and, perhaps, even pestered him so that his forbearance and patience are all the more commendable.

Frequently he was asked for guidance on reading matter, as his reply to Mrs Margaret Gray on 9th May 1961, makes clear:

> For a good ('popular') defence of our position against modern woffle, to fall back on, I know nothing better than G. K. Chesterton's *The Everlasting Man*. Harder reading, but very protective, is Edwyn Bevan's *Symbolism and Belief*. Charles Williams' *He Came Down from Heaven* doesn't suit everyone, but try it.
>
> For meditative and devotional reading (a little bit at a time, more like sucking a lozenge than eating a slice of bread) I suggest *The Imitation of Christ* (astringent) and Traherne's *Centuries of Meditation* (joyous). Also my selection from Macdonald, *George Macdonald: an Anthology*. I can't read Kierkegaard myself, but some people find him helpful.
>
> For Christain morals I suggest my wife's (Joy Davidman) *Smoke on the Mountain*; Gore's *The Sermon on the Mount* and (perhaps) his *Philosophy of the Good Life*. And possibly (but with a grain of salt, for he is too puritanical) William Law's *Serious*

Call to a Devout and Holy Life. I know the very title makes one shudder, but we have both got a lot of shuddering to get through before we're done!

You'll want a mouth-wash for the *imagination*. I'm told that Mauriac's novels (all excellently translated, if your French is rusty) are good, though very severe. Dorothy Sayers' *Man Born to be King* (those broadcast plays) certainly is. So, to me, but not to everyone, are Charles Williams' fantastic novels. *Pilgrim's Progress*, if you ignore some straw-splitting dialogues on Calvinist theology and concentrate on the story, is first-class.[14]

Some of these books had, of course, been important in Lewis's spiritual progress (for example, Chesterton's and Macdonald's). How right he is to say in referring to Law's book, '... but we have both got a lot of shuddering to get through before we're done!' Discipline, suffering, and victory are inextricably intertwined, part of working out our salvation with 'fear and trembling', as St Paul conceived of it.

Equally frequently, people wrote to Lewis asking for advice on purely personal matters;[15] they received careful and balanced answers.[16] These letters are significant also because they show us the other side of Lewis, not the public figure of world renown, but someone who, like the rest of us, feels pain, endures 'chronic temptations', feels frustrated and disillusioned, but for whom God's presence is, in spite of everything, a 'living bright reality'. The spiritual life is often a grinding struggle, but in Lewis's homely and effective illustration,' the bathrooms are all ready, the towels put out, and the clean clothes in the airing cupboard'. In other words, the struggles, the failures and the heart-aches in themselves cannot destroy the inner life if we persist and carry on with the Christian life. Put slightly differently and with another emphasis, it means that God's presence and guiding counsel are always available and at the disposal of the Christian for his or her strengthening.

Religious and devotional questions naturally feature prominently in his letters. In one of them we discover some of the guidelines of his devotional life: (1) he never prayed his main prayers last thing at night; (2) he tried to focus his attention in prayer on God; (3) he did not try to work up emotion by the power of his own will; (4) he prayed without words whenever possible.[17]

The letters indicate that he derived great comfort from prayer.[18] Indeed, he reminds us of the man in Psalm 73 who feels distraught, envious, and bitter, until he experiences the reality of 'God's Grandeur' shooting out to him through prayer, evoking a positive response. For him prayer was an integral part of the Christian's growth in holiness, as is clear in this next extract:

> Oh I *am* glad, I *am* glad. And here's a thing worth recording. Of course I have been praying for you daily, as always, but latterly have found myself doing so with much more concern especially about 2 nights ago, with such a strong feeling how very nice it would be, if God willed, to get a letter from you with good news. And then, as if by magic (indeed it is the whitest magic in the world) the letter comes to-day. Not (lest I should indulge in folly) that your relief had not in fact occurred *before* my prayer, but as if, in tenderness for my puny faith God moved me to pray with especial earnestness just before He was going to give me the thing. How true that our prayers are really His prayers; He speaks to Himself through us. I am also most moved at hearing how you were supported thro' the period of anxiety. For one *is* sometimes tempted to think that if He wanted us to be as un-anxious as the lilies of the field He really might have given us a constitution more like theirs! But then when the need comes *He* carries out in us His otherwise impossible instructions. In fact He always has to do all the things—all the prayers, all the virtues. No new doctrine, but newly come home to me.[19]

There is great honesty too:

> We all go through periods of dryness in our prayers, don't we? I doubt (but ask your *directeur*) whether they are necessarily a bad symptom. I sometimes suspect that what we *feel* to be our best prayers are really our worst; that what we are enjoying is the satisfaction of apparent success, as in executing a dance or reciting a poem. Do our prayers sometimes go wrong because we insist on trying to talk to God when He wants to talk to us? Joy tells me that once, years ago, she was haunted one morning by a feeling that God wanted something of her, a persistent

pressure like the nag of a neglected duty. And till mid-morning she kept on wondering what it was. But the moment she stopped worrying, the answer came through as plain as a spoken voice. It was "I don't want you to *do* anything. I want to *give* you something"; and immediately her heart was full of peace and delight. St. Augustine says "God gives where He finds empty hands". A man whose hands are full of parcels can't receive a gift. Perhaps these parcels are not always sins or earthly cares, but sometimes our own fussy attempts to worship Him in our way. Incidentally, what most often interrupts my own prayers is not great distractions but tiny ones—things one will have to do or avoid in the course of the next hour.[20]

His unashamed admission of 'dryness', when the heavens seem as brass, will strike a chord in many hearts. The last sentence of the second quotation confirms the necessity for shutting the door and getting alone with God (Matthew 6:6). Here Lewis sees this as a purposeful act of the will; it may be the last thing in the world we wish to do at a particular moment, but it must be done.

The letters, too, contain much sound common sense: for example, to avoid psychiatrists unless they are known to be Christians, simply because non-Christian psychiatrists start with the assumption that religion is an illusion which must be cured – they try to be amateur philosophers instead of being professional psychiatrists.

Another striking characterstic of these letters is Lewis's understanding of and sympathy for people going through stressful and disturbing circumstances, including bereavement.[21] He too came to know the heart-ache of losing his wife, and set out his reaction in *A Grief Observed*.

Lewis's dislikes emerge clearly in the letters: the lies that frequently pass for modern journalism, the commercialisation of Christmas and other Christian festivals, excessive summer heat, crowds, machines, some aspects of the welfare state, communism, pride, bigotry, and the need to fast for medical reasons. Equally clear are those facets of life which gave him pleasure: 'the sprinkling of the hoar frost which makes everything sparkle with sugar', the 'empty, silent, dewy, cobwebby' hours of the early morning, the friendship of kindred minds, long walks, and, as he once admitted to a startled reporter, monotony. The letters reveal his generosity, forbearance, and tolerance towards Mrs Moore; he was equally kind and generous with his brother, Warren, who was an alcoholic, frequently going off on drunken orgies in Eire. It was perhaps typical of Warren that he should desert his brother during his final fatal illness during September 1963. He was back at 'The Kilns' though for the afternoon of 22nd November 1963.

For many people the letters are important and interesting especially because of the light they shed on the nature of Lewis's particular style of Christianity. Being *mere*[22] Christianity, it was totally divorced from petty denominational considerations. It was Christianity of a dual nature, hard and tender at one and the same time;[23] one in which God has taken the initiative, and entirely of grace,[24] though the relentlessness of God's pursuit was something he had felt for himself at first hand. It was a Christianity in which the teaching of the Bible was absolutely central,[25] not merely as a 'treasure house of English prose',[26] with literary charm only, but as a source of authority whose claims must be acknowledged and taken seriously.[27] But in his letters it is significant that he does not use the often emotive word 'inerrancy'; rather his view of inspiration is, in Christensen's phrase, that of 'literary inspiration'.[28] Lewis held the Bible to be inspired literature in the sense that it carried the divine message. Biblical literature, human in its origin, had been 'raised by God above itself, qualified by him to serve purposes which of itself would not have been served'. Lewis, then, is not to be classified with those who maintain that unless the Bible is verbally inspired and totally inerrant it cannot be authoritative. Francis Schaeffer, for example, says: 'The issue is whether the Bible is God's verbalized communication to men giving propositionally *true* truth where it touches the cosmos and history or whether it is only in some sense revelational where it touches matters of religion.'[29] Harold Lindsell, in *Battle for the Bible*, asserts: 'However limited may have been their knowledge, and however much they may have erred when they were not writing sacred Scripture, the authors of Scripture, under guidance of the Holy Spirit, were preserved from making factual, historical or scientific errors.'[30] Dr J. I. Packer bases his argument on the nature of God: 'God's Word is affirmed to be infallible because God Himself is infallible; the infallibility of Scripture is simply the infallibility of God speaking. What Scripture says is to be received as the infallible Word of the infallible God, and to assert biblical inerrancy and infallibility is just to confess faith in (1) the divine origin of the Bible and (2) the truthfulness and trustworthiness of God. The value of these terms is they conserve the principle of biblical authority; for statements that are not absolutely true and reliable could not be absolutely authoritative.'[31]

Clearly these views differ markedly in intensity from those of Lewis, but if his differs from evangelical fundamentalism, it is equally obvious that his view of Scripture is a decidedly high one, namely that the Bible is authoritative in all matters of faith, is inspired, and is utterly reliable. On this level the letters are indispensable for evaluating Lewis's beliefs and opinions. It is refreshing to find Lewis willing to admit that he does not know the answer to certain questions of faith:

> I take it as a first principle that we must not interpret any one part of Scripture so that it contradicts other parts, and specially we must not use an apostle's teaching to contradict that of Our Lord. Whatever St. Paul may have meant, we must not reject the parable of the sheep and the goats (Matt. xxv. 30–46). There, you see, there is nothing about Predestination or even about Faith— all depends on works. But how this is to be reconciled with St. Paul's teaching, or with other sayings of Our Lord, I frankly confess I don't know. Even St. Peter, you know, admits that he was stumped by the Pauline Epistles (II Peter. iii. 16–17).[32]

On another level the letters are important because of the glimpses they give of his academic and literary ventures; they contain, for example, an early reference to what eventually became *The Allegory of Love*,[33] while the thinking and research which led to the Oxford *Prolegomena* and then to *The Discarded Image* is revealed in a letter to Sister Penelope.[34] The conception of Screwtape too first appears in a letter to his brother:

After the service was over—one could wish these things came more seasonably—I was struck by an idea for a book which I think might be both useful and entertaining. It would be called 'As one Devil to another' and would consist of letters from an elderly retired devil to a young devil who has just started work on his first 'patient'. The idea would be to give all the psychology of temptation from the other point of view.[35]

The letters also shed light on the reasoning behind some of his key works,[36] contain his definition of the different levels of meaning he was conscious of in *Till We Have Faces*, and explain his understanding of the word 'allegory'.[37] This explanatory note written to an enquirer from Germany is illuminating:

My *Out of the Silent Planet* has no factual basis and is a critique of our own age only as any Christian work is implicitly a critique of any age. I was trying to redeem for genuinely imaginative purposes the form popularly known in this country as 'science-fiction'—I think you call it 'futur-romanz'; just as (*si parva licet componere magnis*) *Hamlet* redeemed the popular revenge play.[38]

In the case of *The Pilgrim's Regress*, it is possible to follow the book from its very beginning right through to its completion and publication. In *April 1930*, a letter to Greeves included religious lyrics which later appeared in the book itself. In *Summer 1932* he refers to the composition of the book during a holiday in Ireland. At *Christmas 1932* he mentions the revision of the manuscript after many consultations with Greeves, and in *May 1933* the book is published.[39]

What is the abiding significance of the three volumes of letters we have looked at briefly in this chapter? Undoubtedly, part of the charm of the letters is that they are so pellucidly written: witty, logical, forceful, colourful, and honest. Lewis's sentences, says Professor Coghill, are homely English'. They are important also because they contain Lewis's uncompromisingly robust defence of orthodox Christianity. But his faith was never narrow or sectarian:

It is right and inevitable that we shd. be much concerned about the salvation of those we love. But we must be careful not to expect or demand that their salvation shd. conform to some ready-made pattern of our own. Some Protestant sects have gone very wrong about this. They have a whole programme of conversion etc. marked out, the same for everyone, and will not believe that anyone can be saved who doesn't go through it 'just so'. But (see the last chapter of my *Problem of Pain*) God has His own way with each soul. There is no evidence that St. John underwent the same kind of 'conversion' as St. Paul. It's not essential to believe in the Devil; and I'm sure a man can get to Heaven without being accurate about Methuselah's age. Also, as Macdonald says, 'the time for *saying* comes seldom, the time for *being* is always here'. What we practise, not (save at rare intervals) what we preach, is usually our great contribution to the conversion of others.[40]

Taken together with his published works, they may be regarded as part of that 'special mission' Lewis performed for those who were 'slowly finding their way towards some sort of Christian orthodoxy'. Whatever their backgrounds, such people were looking for a faith which was firmly fixed in the mainstream of the Christian tradition, but which was not obscurely fundamentalist in its attitude to intellect, knowledge, and imagination. As *The Times* obituary said: 'C. S. Lewis stood out as an encouragement and an example to all those who feel that there is less and less room in the world for imaginative faith.'

These letters may also be regarded as 'parallel autobiography', preserving as they do much detail about Lewis's life. Their importance appears in the extensive use made of them by Roger Green and Walter Hooper in the official biography. The letters offer deep insights into the character, temperament, and personality of a remarkable man of God. Finally a question: why did Lewis devote so much time and effort to answering his letters, especially those dealing with Christian matters. Professor Clyde Kilby's answer cannot be bettered:

The main cause was that Lewis believed that taking time out to answer or encourage another Christian was both a humbling of one's talents before the Lord and also as much the work of the Holy Spirit as producing a book.[41]

CHAPTER SEVEN

An Appraisal

Much has been written about the life, friends, habits, abilities and career of Lewis during the past twenty years or so, and doubtless his published works will continue to attract many different categories of people in the future.

The need now is for a *balanced approach* both to his achievements and character. The date of his death is long past. Acquaintances and friends, such as Coghill and Tolkien, have fallen victim to life's only real certainty. The BBC magazine, *The Listener*, recognised in 1981 that the time was ripe for a 're-assessment' of his Narnia books. We may ask two questions: (1) What are the significant aspects of his life and work? (2) What is his reputation mid-way through the eighties?

In this chapter we shall formulate some conclusions about his character, his scholarly works, and finally his Christian publications.

Lewis was an unusual and complex person. A highly imaginative and precocious child, he grew into a talented and able young man who scorned the rigidity of the British public school system. In all probability Malvern College was no worse than other public schools at the beginning of the twentieth century, but Lewis obviously required greater intellectual stimulation and mature comradeship than he found there. He had a deep need for the friendship of those who shared his literary and poetic interests, especially in such matters as 'joy' and 'myth'. At this time he seems to have had few close friends, Arthur Greeves being a notable exception.

Lewis was a paradoxical person in many ways. Possessed of a phenomenal memory, he frequently forgot about the books and articles he had written. He hated letter-writing – the three volumes of his letters published since his death contain innumerable references to the burden of his 'mails' which pursued him wherever he went – yet spent large tracts of time answering letters from people from all over the world in a patient and serious way. A good example is the letter he wrote to a clergyman who had married Lewis and Joy but who later wrote asking for their prayers. In his reply, Lewis assured the despondent priest of his prayers and asked if he could help, ending his letter like this:

> God bless you both. I shall have no need to 'remind' myself to remember you. Let us have news as soon as there is any.
> If you find (some do) that mental anguish produces an inclination to eat more—paradoxical but it can—I should jolly well do so!

He disliked the cult of the personality, yet apparently played the rôle of the Grand Old Man at Cambridge with some relish and amusement. He was gentle and tactful with many people much less gifted than himself but was frequently heavy-handed and bullying in debate; robustness may be an appropriate word here, but even if this word is used, it is indisputable that many of his students – especially those of limited ability and knowledge – felt intimidated and possibly threatened by him.

But perhaps most paradoxical of all were his dealings with Mrs Moore and with Joy Davidman. Mrs Moore was an extremely difficult person who shared none of Lewis's intellectual pursuits or concerns, and who frequently demanded help from him with such routine matters as making marmalade, spring-cleaning, and packing. In his journal for March 1924 he says that when occupied with domestic drudgery he had kept his temper 'nearly all the time'. Yet, in spite of all this, he permitted her to interfere with academic work, often on the flimsiest of pretexts. His patience in these circumstances was nothing less than saintly. And why? Only, it appears, because he had promised his friend Paddy Moore to look after his mother in the event of Moore's death in the First World War. Certainly Lewis fulfilled his promise far beyond the bounds of ordinary kindess and morality right through to the end of her life. The explanation of his biographers is both plausible and attractive: 'His affection for Mrs Moore – his infatuation, as it seemed to his friends and even to his brother who knew him more intimately than any of them – may have started with that incomprehensible passion which attractive middle-age women seem occasionally to inspire in susceptible youth: but it very soon turned from the desire for a mistress into the creation of a mother-substitute – in many ways a father-substitute also.'[3] In *The Inklings* Humphrey Carpenter describes Lewis's strange involvement with Mrs Moore and recounts that when Warren Lewis asked his brother about the relationship – and he did so once only – he was told quite firmly to mind his own business. While it is highly unlikely that Mrs Moore was ever Lewis's mistress, his friendship with her could never have been, in Carpenter's words, 'entirely respectable'.[4] In fact, it was a completely illogical relationship, and placed a strain not only upon his domestic peace and harmony, but also, especially in the latter years of Mrs Moore's life, upon his financial resources.

It does seem however to imply a susceptibility for 'lame ducks', because he entered into another paradoxical situation years later with Joy Davidman, who invaded his masculine world with dramatic and complicating effect. Hooper is right to describe their relationship as 'bittersweet';[5] it could scarcely have been anything else. It progressed through friendship, in the first instance, to an act of kindness – he married her on 23rd April 1956 merely to secure her the rights and protection of British citizenship: this was a civil and legal contract only. Later, friendship and kindness were replaced by love, and he married her, in a ceremony presided over by a priest, on 21st March 1957. If his relationship with Joy was now one of love, it cannot be denied that it was also controversial. As a divorcee she could not – and did not – receive the official blessing of the Church of England, but eventually someone was prevailed upon to perform the ceremony. Naturally his brother had doubts about such a union, but it was Tolkien, of all Lewis's friends, who found the marriage most upsetting. His biographer records Tolkien's puzzlement and anger at this event.[6] Why did Tolkien react in this manner? Carpenter says: 'Some of his feelings may be explained by the fact that she had been divorced from her first husband before she married Lewis, some by resentment of Lewis's expectation that his friends should pay court to his new wife – whereas in the thirties Lewis, very much the bachelor, had liked to ignore the fact that his friends had wives to go home to.'[7] The real reason was this : 'Tolkien felt betrayed by the marriage, resented the intrusion of a woman into his friendship with Lewis'.[8] Thereafter Tolkien was never so intimately friendly. Another contributory factor in Tolkien's unfavourable reaction was the fact that he heard of the marriage in church only at second-hand. Coghill strikes a much gentler, more accepting note in *Light on C. S. Lewis* by mentioning an incident which occurred not long after the marriage:

> When he brought his wife to lunch with me, he said to me, looking at her across the grassy quadrangle, 'I never expected to have, in my sixties, the happiness that passed me by in my twenties.' It was then that he told me of having been allowed to accept her pain.
>
> 'You mean' (I said) 'that her pain left her, and that you felt it for her in your body?'
>
> 'Yes,' he said, 'in my legs. It was crippling. But it relieved hers.'[9]

Only three years were vouchsafed to Lewis and Joy, and on 13th July 1960 she died after an unavailing and courageous fight against cancer. Lewis had known she was desperately ill when he married her, but this did not make her death any easier for him to bear, and in one of his letters he referred to the 'apparent unreality'[10] of his life since she died. That he felt sharp grief is clear not only from his letters, but supremely in *A Grief Observed*, which was published originally under the pseudonym of N. W. Clerk, his identity being revealed only after his own death three years later.

The title has several levels of meaning: there is Lewis's perfectly genuine grief after Joy's death; then there is the analysis of that feeling as it affected him both internally and in terms of external behaviour. It is a powerful, highly sophisticated and intellectual work: it is in fact anything but an 'artless' work, but this last sentence must not be construed to mean that the feelings he describes and evaluates were bogus or insincere. Lewis felt her death, after a pitifully short marriage, very keenly indeed; he confessed to being like a 'sleep-walker'. So in this book he worked out his grief in an effort to understand it. He identifies, on a purely human level, feelings of fear, grinding loneliness, the sudden piercing jabs of 'red-hot memory', the pathos, the laziness, embarrassment, the desire for anonymity and obscurity – in short, the stark and awful aftermath of bereavement. He found himself growing impatient with people who claim death does not matter: 'There is death. And whatever matters has consequences, and it and they are irrevocable and irreversible. You might as well say that birth doesn't matter.' As for 'getting over the whole thing', he felt that such words were themselves meaningless. Metaphorically he described his desire that presently he would be given a wooden leg to take the weight of grief, but felt nevertheless that he would not be as he put it, 'a biped again'.[11] In addition, he felt deep forebodings about the future – he recalled that his Mother, Father, and now Joy had all been struck down by cancer and he naturally wondered who would be 'next in the queue'.[12] Without any worthwhile photograph of Joy in his possession he felt a not unusual inability to recall her face distinctly in his imagination, though her voice was vivid and vibrant to him. Perhaps most of all he missed the 'rough, sharp, cleansing tang of her otherness',[13] and the reality that was their marriage.[14]

Lewis found no easy relief for his agony, not even, perhaps especially not, in religion as a comforting, consoling force. He was prepared to listen to the 'truth' of religion, would accede submissively to the 'duty' of religion, but would not listen to talk of the 'consolations' of religion.[15] At this time he considered all talk about joyful family reunions taking place on 'the further shore' as, at best unscriptural, at worst, false. To him there remained only the intangible, the unsatisfactory: 'no answer'. He was aware of the iron curtain, the locked door, the vacuum: 'absolute zero'.[16] Prayer too was futile, and when he tried to pray he was hesitant, bewildered, amazed by all that had happened. His dominant feeling was of unreality: 'of speaking into a vacuum about a nonentity'.[17] He wrote to an American lady: 'The moments at which you call most desperately and clamorously to God for help are precisely those when you seem to get none.'[18] This 'curious discovery', as he termed it, was linked to another realisation: 'The moments at which I feel nearest to Joy are precisely those when I mourn her least.'[19] Later, a change occurred:

> Suddenly at the very moment when, so far, I mourned H. least, I remembered her best. Indeed it was something (almost) better than memory; an instantaneous, unanswerable impression. To say it was like a meeting would be going too far. Yet there was that in it which tempts one to use those words. It was as if the lifting of the sorrow removed a barrier.[20]

Still later, Joy seemed to meet him everywhere. 'Meet' is, perhaps, too strong a word, but the experience involved more than a voice or an apparition. It was, rather, 'a sort of unobtrusive but massive sense that she is, just as much as ever, a fact to be taken into account'.[21] Still later he felt 'better', though this was accompanied by a sort 'of shame', and the feeling that perhaps he was under an obligation to 'cherish and foment' his unhappiness.[22] He analysed the reason for this as being vanity – the wish to prove to himself that he belonged to that rare collection of people who were 'lovers on the grand scale, tragic heroes'.[23] The realisation dawned that passionate grief, far from linking him with the dead, actually separated him from Joy. Then came the confidence to face the old haunts, the places he had visited with her. Gradually he experienced healing and acceptance, even of the unanswerable questions, and he realised that

recording his tortured and injured feelings had become a
'defence again;t total collapse', a safety-valve for him.[24] *A
Grief Observed* ends like this (p. 60): 'How wicked it would
be, if we could, to call the dead back. She said not to me but
to the chaplain, "I am at peace with God." She smiled, but
not at me. *Poi si torno all eterna fontana'* ("Then she turned to
the eternal fountain" – a reference to Dante and Beatrice.)

So much for Lewis's personal character and behaviour.
What of his achievement as a scholar? There is little doubt
that his academic work will ensure for him a lasting memory
and significance. Whatever dictionary definition we select,
Lewis was a scholar. He was certainly: 'a person who has
acquired experience or information; a learned man.' He had
undergone 'a training in accuracy and critical method' and
[possessed] a mastery of some subject.' He had in a narrower
sense – 'a minute knowledge and mastery of the refinement
of the classical languages'. Three volumes in particular
exemplify Lewis the critic and scholar: they are, in chronological order, *The Allegory of Love* (1936), *A Preface to Paradise
Lost* (1942), and *English Literature in the Sixteenth-Century
Excluding Drama* (1954).

The sub-title of the first of these volumes, 'A Study in
Medieval Tradition', indicates the scope and intention of the
work, which entailed prodigious preparatory reading, over
several years. It pin-points Lewis's great and abiding interest: medieval studies. He pursues his theme in a two-fold
way: first he traces the rise and progress of the sentiment
called 'Courtly Love', and secondly he analyses the progress
of the allegorical method from the eleventh century to the
sixteenth century. The initial reference to this work is found
in a letter he wrote to his brother in July 1928: 'The actual
book is about medieval love poetry and the medieval idea of
love, which is a very paradoxical business when you go into
it: for on the one hand it is extremely super-sensual and
refined, and on the other hand it is an absolute point of
honour that the lady should be someone else's wife, as
Dante and Beatrice, Lancelot and Guinevere etc.'[25]

Detailed chapters are devoted to 'The Romance of the
Rose' and 'The Faerie Queene', as well as to such poets as
Chaucer and Gower. Easy familiarity with frequently com-

plex material is apparent on every page, and the *Observer* reviewer commented in glowing terms: 'Out of the multitudes of volumes on literary criticism there arises once or twice in a generation a truly great work. Such I believe is this study by Mr C. S. Lewis.' The *Times Educational Supplement* reviewer praised in particular Lewis's appreciation of Chaucer's 'Troilus and Criseyde', as of 'the very highest quality', while *Modern Language Notes* considered it 'a really outstanding contribution to medieval studies'. These verdicts have been substantiated and endorsed down through the years by other critics and scholars. Professor Coghill felt that *The Allegory of Love* was a 'magistral book', but commented perfectly fairly, 'It may be that the *Chronicles of Narnia* may outlive *The Allegory of Love*, and *Perelandra* outlive them both. Few works of learning and criticism survive a hundred years; what was learned to know in 1950 will be expected of scholarship candidates in 2000; new things will be discovered, old notions disproved, other critical values asserted; but a piece of genuine imagination in fiction may have a long life.'[26]

Lewis's achievement in this work is many-sided. He illuminated, in Coghill's words, 'a whole way of sexual feeling',[27] and in a manner that blended the historical with the imaginative. It is obligatory reading for all those interested in the medieval world, and the so-called 'introductions' to Chaucer rely very heavily on it for their sections on 'Courtly Love'. Few have been obliged to disagree with Lewis's study, or with the conservatively expressed view of his biographers that *The Allegory of Love* established him as a 'first-rate scholar and writer of exceptional imaginative power'.[28]

An incidental result of this work was that it brought him into contact with Charles Williams, then a member of the editorial staff at the Oxford University Press, who wrote to Lewis: 'I regard your book as practically the only one I have ever come across, since Dante, that shows the slightest understanding of what this very peculiar identity of love and religion means.'[29] A warm friendship between the two men was forged, and Williams become one of Lewis's intimates and a member of 'The Inklings'. Williams's untimely death affected Lewis deeply; he refers in a letter to his being acquainted with grief through the death of his 'great friend Charles Williams', whom he also calls his 'friend of friends'.[30] Apart from what has already been said, *The Allegory of Love* was a pioneering work which led to increased understanding of the complex inter-relationship between love and religion.

A Preface to Paradise Lost has prompted more disagreement. To grasp Lewis's intention and method in this book, it is necessary to relate it to the 'Milton Controversy' which has raged with considerable intensity and acrimony during the twentieth century. The reputation of literary figures can fluctuate enormously, and Milton is no exception.[31] During his own life-time, in spite of his intense conviction regarding his rôle as a poet in society, he was in all probability an obscure figure. Only after his death did his reputation begin to grow, until by 1686 Dryden could say in his 'Epigram on Milton':

Three poets, in three distant ages born,
Greece, Italy, and England did adorn.
The first in loftiness of thought surpass'd,
The next in majesty, in both the last:
The force of Nature could no farther go;
To make a third, she join'd the former two.

By the beginning of the nineteenth century, his stock as a poet was extremely high. Wordsworth's well-known sonnet expressed his conviction that England 'hath need of thee'.[32]

It was equally high half-way through the nineteenth-century when Tennyson described him as a 'mighty mouth'd inventor of harmonies ... a name to resound for ages'.[33]

Coleridge's description of Milton as Shakespeare's 'compeer not rival' aptly sums up the prevailing critical opinion of two centuries. But the early part of the twentieth-century saw a marked turning-point as Milton's work (by which *Paradise Lost* is primarily meant) came under increasing attack; the debunking process had begun. Essentially two charges were levelled against him. The first was that his poetic style was inherently deficient because of its 'artificiality'. Secondly, his influence on English poetry and the English language was perceived as detrimental.[34] Prominent in this attack was T. S. Eliot, who claimed that 'Milton's poetry could only be an influence for the worse, upon any poet whatever'. He affirmed that 'Milton's bad influence may be traced much further than the eighteenth-century, and much further upon bad poets'.[35] Middleton Murry, who approached Milton after a serious study of Keats's poetry, felt, like Keats, that 'to be influenced beyond a certain point by Milton's art, ... dammed the creative flow of the English genius in and through itself. ... To pass under the spell of Milton is to be condemned to imitate him. It is quite different with Shakespeare. Shakespeare baffles and liberates; Milton is perspicuous and constrict.'[36] Ezra Pound felt that Milton ranked with minor poets such as Drummond of Hawthornden rather than with Shakespeare; only stupidity would categorise Milton with 'the Bard'.[37] Of more substance are the views of F. R. Leavis who claimed, in *Revaluation: Tradition and Development in English Poetry*, that 'Milton's dislodgement', after 'two centuries of dominance', had been 'effected with remarkably little fuss'. ... 'In the end we find ourselves protesting – protesting against the routine gesture, the heavy fall, of the verse, flinching from the foreseen thud that comes so inevitably, and, at last, irresistibly: for reading *Paradise Lost* is a matter of resisting, of standing up against, the verse-movement, of subduing it into something tolerably like sensitiveness, and in the end our resistance is worn down; we surrender to the inescapable monotony of the ritual.'[38] Other writers, including A. J. A. Waldock, refer to serious weaknesses in the narrative in *Paradise Lost*.

Among Milton's defenders was Lewis with his *Preface*. The problem, as he saw it, was that 'Milton criticism is lost in misunderstanding.' The critics and the poet were at cross-purposes. He concluded bluntly that the detractors 'did not see what the poem was about'. In a section headed, 'Is Criticism Possible?', he argues shrewdly against T. S. Eliot's view that the only 'jury of judgement' consists of the best contemporary poets currently practising.

Mr Eliot is ready to accept the verdict of the best contemporary poets on his criticism. But how does *he* recognize them as poets? Clearly, because he is a poet himself; for if he is not, his opinion is worthless. At the basis of his whole critical edifice, then, lies the judgement "I am a poet." But this is a critical judgement. It therefore follows that when Mr Eliot asks himself, "Am I a poet?" he has to *assume* the answer "I am" before he can *find* the answer "I am"; for the answer, being a piece of criticism, is valuable only *if* he is a poet. He is thus compelled to beg the question before he can get started at all. Similarly Mr Auden and Mr Pound must beg the question before *they* get started. But since no man of high intellectual honour can base his thought on an exposed *petitio* the real result is that no such man can criticize poetry at all, neither his own poetry nor that of his neighbour. The republic of letters resolves itself into an aggregate of uncommunicating and unwindowed monads; each has unawares crowned and mitred himself Pope and King of Pointland. (pp 9–10)

Lewis's defence is quite simply this: that where the qualities of *Paradise Lost* were 'remote and artificial', such qualities were required by its epic form. Ultimately Lewis saw it as a question of genre and maintained that the critical question is whether the style of *Paradise Lost* conforms to the laws of its particular poetic genre, and not whether it lacks 'flexibility or rhythmic variety'. In his view Milton's style was simply the appropriate one for his subject. He answered the charge brought against Milton's diction, syntax and use of Latin idioms by claiming that the particular poetic diction of *Paradise Lost* was speech common in Milton's time, and that 'while Milton's Latin constructions in one way tighten up our language, in another way they make it more fluid. A fixed order of words is the price – an all but ruinous price – which English pays for being uninflected. The Miltonic constructions enable the poet to depart, in some degree, from this fixed order and thus drop the ideas into his sentence in any order he choses.'[39]

Lewis's *Preface* goes to the very heart of the Milton controversy, and it remains a volume of permanent importance for scholars of the Puritan-poet, though naturally there are other scholars who disagree with his interpretation. One such person is Christopher Ricks, who has written what is arguably the best defence of Milton's style in a book entitled *Milton's Grand Style*. Ricks considers Lewis to be the most influential of all the 'traditionalists' but regrets the fact that 'Mr Lewis hands the argument over at once to the philosopher and the theologian' – a judicious and well-founded criticism. Nevertheless, he feels that Lewis is excellent in his comments on 'style' and wishes he had written at greater length on this subject. Unlike Lewis, Ricks analyses Milton's style in considerable detail. He concludes: 'Milton's Grand Style is delicately suggestive, very much more flexible and supple than is sometimes thought. ... At its very best, Milton's style is remarkable for its simultaneous combination of what is energetically strong with what is winning soft and amiably mild'.[40] None of this, however, alters the general view of Lewis's *Preface* as being a study of considerable importance; obligatory reading for all who wish to take Milton seriously.

But the *Preface* does not only deal with Milton's style. It is also very much concerned with criticisms of Milton's theology, especially his view of the Fall, his supposed Arianism in *Paradise Lost*, and his portrayal of Satan.

Regarding the first of these, Lewis concludes that 'The Fall is simply and solely Disobedience – doing what you have been told not to do: and it results from Pride – from being too big for your boots, forgetting your place, thinking that you are God. This is what St Augustine thinks and what (to the best of my knowledge) the Church has always taught'. Readers who cannot be interested in this aspect of Milton's epic 'can't be interested in *Paradise Lost*'. Here Lewis's qualifying parenthesis ('to the best of my knowledge') is wise, because, in fact, this is not the view of the Eastern branch of the Church. Nevertheless, it is the view adopted by Milton from the first line of his poem.

As far as the second of these, issues is concerned, Lewis deals with it in 'The Theology of Paradise Lost' (section 12). Here he comes into conflict with Professor Saurat who had suggested that the heresy of Arianism is to be found in Book 5, line 603 of *Paradise Lost*: 'This day I begot whom I declare. My onely Son'. The literal meaning of this line is that the

Son of God was created *after* the angels. Lewis, however, shows that this could not be so in *Paradise Lost*, because Book 3 line 390 declares that 'God *created* the angels by the agency of the Son'. The same assertion occurs in Book 5 line 835, when Abdiel refutes Satan's attacks. Lewis also demonstrates that Milton's *De Doctrina* gives the clue to the meaning of the word *beget*: literally it refers to the reproduction of the Son; metaphorically it alludes to his exaltation. This is how Lewis concludes the whole matter:

> '"This day I have begot" must mean "This day I have exalted", for otherwise it is inconsistent with the rest of the poem. And if this is so, we admit that Milton's Arianism is not asserted in *Paradise Lost* (p. 85).

Finally, what of the charge, made by William Blake, for example, that 'Milton was of the devil's party without knowing it'? Did the poet, himself a rebel against the authority of Charles I, portray Satan, the arch-rebel, as a heroic character? Lewis distinguishes two ways of interpreting this viewpoint. It may imply that Milton's presentation is a poetical achievement of a magnificent order which gains the attention of readers and excites their admiration. Alternatively, it may mean that Milton's Satan is or perhaps ought to be 'an object of admiration and sympathy, conscious or unconscious, on the part of the poet or his readers or both' (p. 92). Only in modern times, he says, has the first of these propositions been denied, whereas the second had never been affirmed before Blake and Shelley. Lewis sees Milton's Satan as a perceptive portrayal of evil. Satan combines an active, subtle and penetrating intellect with an 'incapacity to understand anything' (p. 96). To admire Satan is to vote for a 'world of misery ... a world of lies and propaganda, of wishful thinking, of incessant autobiography' (p. 100). Ultimately, Lewis asserts, Satan 'is an ass' – he is not romantic or heroic, he is morally reprehensible and absurd; his grotesqueness made all the more horrible and dangerous by the fact that he is an inveterate liar. Indeed, Lewis says, because Satan lies consistently about everything in *Paradise Lost*, we cannot distinguish 'his conscious lies from the blindness he has almost willingly imposed on himself'.

Nor is there any tension in Lewis's mind between Satan's essential characteristics and the claim that of all Milton's characters Satan is 'the best drawn'. In fact, the two things are intimately related:

> The Satan in Milton enables him to draw the character well just as the Satan in us enables us to receive it. Not as Milton, but as man, he has trodden the burning marl, pursued vain war with heaven, and turned aside with leer malign. A fallen man *is* very like a fallen angel (p. 99).

Thus, the Satanic predicament can never be comic for us:

> It is too near us: and doubtless Milton expected all readers to perceive that in the long run either the Satanic predicament or else the delighted obedience of Messiah, of Abdiel, of Adam, and of Eve, must be their own. It is therefore right to say that Milton has put much of himself into Satan; but it is unwarrantable to conclude that he was pleased with that part of himself or expected us to be pleased. Because he was, like the rest of us, damnable, it does not follow that he was, like Satan, damned (p.99).

After all, as Lewis indicates, to create a character who is worse than ourselves, requires only one ingredient: an imaginative release from control of those passions 'which, in real life, are always straining at the leash'. His telling analogy at this point in his argument is that the Satan, the Iago, the Becky Sharp that resides in every person is only too anxious to slip the leash and demonstrate itself. Whether or not we allow this to happen is a question of personal choice. Lewis's argument here is completely at one with his Christian teaching and apologetics.

The very presentation of these choices constitutes for Lewis the seriousness of *Paradise Lost*: it may also explain why the controversy between Lewis and Leavis regarding Milton wasn't simply caused by disagreement over the Puritan-poet's style and language. Aeschliman agrees:

Underneath what seems to be a merely aesthetic disagreement
is the real root of the antagonism: with Dante and Spencer,
Milton stands among the great and explicitly theological poets,
and it is over theology that Lewis and Leavis parted ways.[42]

The last of Lewis's academic works to call for our attention is
English Literature in the Sixteenth-Century Excluding Drama,
which forms part of the 'Oxford History of English Literature Series' (O.H.E.L.). The opening paragraph shows Lewis
at his best and indicates his perspective:

The rough outline of our literary history in the sixteenth century
is not very difficult to grasp. At the beginning we find a
literature still medieval in form and spirit. In Scotland it shows
the highest level of technical brilliance: in England it has for
many years been dull, feeble, and incompetent. As the century
proceeds, new influences arise: changes in our knowledge of
antiquity, new poetry from Italy and France, new theology, new
movements in philosophy or science. As these increase, though
not necessarily because of them, the Scotch literature is almost
completely destroyed. In England the characteristic disease of
late medieval poetry, its metrical disorder, is healed: but replaced, for the most part, by a lifeless and laboured regularity to
which some ears might prefer the vagaries of Lydgate. There is
hardly any sign of a new inspiration. Except for the songs of
Wyatt, whose deepest roots are medieval, and the prose of the
Prayer Book, which is mostly translation, authors seem to have
forgotten the lessons which had been mastered in the Middle
Ages and learned little in their stead. Their prose is clumsy,
monotonous, garrulous; their verse either astonishingly tame
and cold or, if it attempts to rise, the coarsest fustian. In both
mediums we come to dread a certain ruthless emphasis;
bludgeon-work. Nothing is light, or tender, or fresh. All the
authors write like elderly men. The mid-century is an earnest,
heavy-handed, commonplace age: a drab age. Then, in the last
quarter of the century, the unpredictable happens. With start-
ling suddenness we ascend. Fantasy, conceit, paradox, colour,
incantation return. Youth returns. The fine frenzies of ideal love
and ideal war are readmitted. Sidney, Spenser, Shakespeare,
Hooker—even, in a way, Lyly—display what is almost a new
culture: that culture which was to last through most of the
seventeenth century and to enrich the very meanings of the
words *English* and *Aristocracy*. Nothing in the earlier history of

our period would have enabled the sharpest observer to foresee this transformation.

The pinnacles of the work are Lewis's treatment of the medieval literature of Scotland, and the literary output of such people as Hooker, Spenser, and Sydney, while others like Tyndale are re-assessed. Two other features – an extensive bibliography and a detailed chronological table – made the original edition an especially valuable contribution to our knowledge and understanding of the period. Professor Frank Kermode expressed the opinion that Lewis had written a 'book in a great tradition, a book almost overwhelmingly rich and assured'. It is a formidable work if only for the amount of reading required to write it. But it has not received the critical acclaim accorded the two volumes referred to above. One reason for this, in Helen Gardner's view, is that 'the book is marred throughout by an insistent polemical purpose, expressed in the title of its first chapter "New Learning and New Ignorance"'. But she adds that it is brilliantly written and is 'compulsorily readable, and constantly illuminated by sentences that are as true as they are witty'.[43]

What, in conclusion, are Lewis's qualities as a critic and scholar? His natural intelligence and analytic skill were, of course, outstanding, but over and beyond these we recognise his enthusiasm. For Lewis reading was never work, and one recalls his snort of disapproval, in *An Experiment in Criticism*, for those who might be expected to have a profound and permanent appreciation of literature but in reality have nothing of the sort.

> I well remember the snub I once got from a man to whom, as we came away from an examiners' meeting, I tactlessly mentioned a great poet on whom several candidates had written answers. His attitude (I've forgotten the words) might be expressed in the form 'Good God, man, do you want to go on *after hours*? Didn't you hear the hooter blow?' (p. 7)

His scholarly works – not only the ones referred to earlier – reveal his ability to obtain a clear grasp of the facts and then to convey that information precisely and coherently. This talent for identifying the essence of a writer's work is consistently illustrated throughout his O.H.E.L. volume, together with his skill in comparing two different aspects of a poet's work. Few scholars can rival his capacity for telling generalisations.

His characteristic robustness appears in his verdict on William Webbe's work as a critic[44]:

'William Webbe is in a class by himself, uniquely bad. His discourse of English Poetry (1586) displays an ignorance even then hardly credible. He is a perfect specimen of the literary "hanger on" who without knowledge, sensibility, or sense volunteers support for all that his betters are doing when they are least wise and praises all who are already popular.'

Other qualities shown in his academic works include independence of judgement, imagination, and stylistic grace. Coghill comments that these abound with 'sentences that a critical writer may envy'. Penetration, sensitivity, readability are all present in a marked degree in his literary criticism, to read which convinces us of what Lewis himself called the 'enormous extension of our being which we owe to our authors'.

Finally, Lewis will be remembered as a modern hero of the faith. His conversion in 1929, to theism in the first instance, did not occur without a struggle – he called himself the 'most reluctant convert in all England'. Full Christian belief came later, and from that time onwards he took, with absolute seriousness, the words and teaching of Christ as a guide for his everyday life. Walter Hooper has referred to Lewis as the 'most thoroughly converted man' he had ever encountered. For Lewis Christianity was not something introduced into the vacuum left over after his intellectual and creative yearnings had been satisfied: it was the motivating force of his life. Not religion certainly, for in *Letters to Malcolm* he refers to a man who had substituted religion for God, and says that 'even in this present life there is danger in the very concept of *religion*. It carries the suggestion that this is one more department of life, an extra department added to the economic, the social, the intellectual, the

recreational, and all the rest'.[45] Aware of the contrast between religion and Christianity, he viewed the conflict
between God and the Devil in every sense as a battle: 'There
is no neutral ground in the universe: every square inch,
every split second, is claimed by God and counter-claimed
by Satan'.[46]

Although his own faith was deeply grounded and intense
and although he devoted much time to encouraging others,
Lewis did not force his faith on people. Sheldon Vanauken
records that on the first occasion when he dined with Lewis
at Magdalen College (just after he had come to faith in
Christ), Lewis suggested it would be better to avoid discussing Christian matters in Hall or in the Common Room since
he knew that some of the other Fellows were unhappy about
his Christian vocation and attitudes.[47]

Clyde Kilby has observed that Lewis's Christian books are
unified and cohesive; they are in fact 'remarkably of a piece'.
Kilby identifies various motifs, including the one of battle
mentioned above, also the need for choice between hell and
heaven, for obedience to God and the obligation upon
Christians to put self to death.[46] There were other aspects of
Christian teaching on which he laid particular stress. He
emphasised that man was made in the image of God;
though fallen and flawed, he has a deep thirst within him
that only God can satisfy; but that when one looks to Christ,
one will find him, 'and with Him everything else thrown in'.
To argue against Christ is to argue against the very power
that enables us to argue at all; to find Christ is to find reality;
man is the object of the highest and most marvellous love.
He saw Christianity as essentially practical and often demanding: if Christ is to be the operative force and influence,
pride has to be overcome and freedom may be obtained only
through obedience, pleasure through humility and personality through unity. In the last resort it is a question not of
our feelings but of our wills, surrendering ourselves to our
Creator in a process that ends only when the Christian
reaches heaven. Of this he says in *The Weight of Glory*:[48]

The promises of Scripture may very roughly be reduced to five
heads. It is promised, firstly, that we shall be with Christ;

secondly, that we shall be like Him; thirdly, with an enormous wealth of imagery, that we shall have glory; fourthly, that we shall, in some sense, be fed or feasted or entertained; and, finally, that we shall have some sort of official position in the universe – ruling cities, judging angels, being pillars of God's temple.

Yearly sales of Lewis's works approach two million volumes in Britain and America, which is abundant proof of his enduring popularity. Why should this be so? In a perceptive critique, Michael Aeschliman suggests it is because Lewis aimed his arguments at the common man. He refers to Lewis's assumption that almost all good men who have ever thought honestly share universal convictions which may differ in detail but not in substance; and to his firm belief in the fund of common sense of men 'throughout history'. Aeschliman underlines Lewis's unshakeable conviction that the amorality, atheism, and agnosticism of the twentieth-century constitute an aberration within this historical tradition of common sense as evidenced by Aristotle, Augustine, Aquinas, Samuel Johnson, and G. K. Chesterton.

To the task of showing 'the immeasurable worth of man ... not a thing, but an essence, a soul', Lewis brought the conviction that propagating religion should not be esoteric nor mystical nor academic, but should involve the resources of a fertile and creative imagination, a finely honed historical imagination, and, of course, enormous intellectual power. In *C. S. Lewis At The Breakfast Table*, Dom Bede Griffiths makes a similar point: that the immense force of Lewis's Christian apologetics is due not only to the combination of 'rigorous critical intellect' with 'rich poetic imagination', but to his capacity 'to speak to the common man and see into the hidden motives in the heart of everyman' (p. 17).

Reading Lewis's presentation of Christian doctrines and related ethical behaviour is both demanding and comforting. In the twenty-odd years since his death nobody has shown a capacity to defend Christianity with such authority and power, devastating logic and complete conviction, nor with such grace and style. Although to read Lewis is not always to agree with him, disagreeing with him is far more rewarding than with the pious platitudes that have so often masqueraded as arguments for Christian orthodoxy. Perhaps nobody can fully replace the man whom Charles Moorman described as a 'cocktail party *advocatus Christi*'.[50]

Notes

The following abbreviations are used in these notes:

AEIC   – *An Experiment in Criticism* (Cambridge University Press, 1961)

AGO   – *A Grief Observed* (Faber and Faber, 1961)

AMA   – *A Mind Awake*, edited by Clyde Kilby (Geoffrey Bles, London 1968)

AOM   – *The Abolition of Man* (Fount Paperbacks, 1978)

Biog   – *C. S. Lewis: A Biography*, by Roger Lancelyn Green and Walter Hooper (Collins, London 1974)

CR   – *Christian Reflections*, edited by Walter Hooper (Geoffrey Bles, London 1967)

FL   – *The Four Loves* (Fontana, 1960)

FS   – *Fern-seed and Elephants and other essays on Christianity*, edited by Walter Hooper (Fontana, 1975)

LAL   – *Letters To An American Lady*, edited by Clyde Kilby (Hodder and Stoughton, 1967)

LL   – *The Letters of C. S. Lewis*, edited by W. H. Lewis (Geoffrey Bles, London 1966)

MC   – *Mere Christianity* (Fontana Books, 1952)

OTSP   – *Out of the Silent Planet* (Pan Books, 1952)

P   – *Poems*, edited by Walter Hooper (Geoffrey Bles, London 1964)

Per   – *Voyage to Venus [Perelandra]* (Pan Books, 1953)

POP   – *The Problem of Pain* (Geoffrey Bles, 1942)

SBJ   – *Surprised by Joy* (Geoffrey Bles, London 1955)

SLE   – *Selected Literary Essays*, edited by edited by Walter Hooper (Cambridge University Press, 1969)

TAFP   – *They Asked for a Paper* (Geoffrey Bles, London 1962)

TGD   – *The Great Divorce* (Geoffrey Bles, London 1946)

THS   – *That Hideous Strength* (Pan Books, 1955)

TPR   – *The Pilgrim's Regress* (Collins, Fount Paperbacks, 1978)

TSC   – *The Silver Chair* (Puffin Books, 1965)

TSL   – *The Screwtape Letters* (Fontana, 1942)

TST   – *They Stand Together: The Letters of C. S. Lewis to Arthur Greeves (1914–63)*, edited by Walter Hooper (Collins, 1979)

TLWW   – *The Lion, the Witch, and the Wardrobe* (Penguin Books, 1959)

Un   – *Undeceptions: Essays on Theology and Ethics*, edited by Walter Hooper (Geoffrey Bles, London 1971)

VDT   – *The Voyage of the Dawn Treader* (Puffin Books, 1965)
(The volumes referred to above were the ones used in the writing of this work).

Chapter One INTRODUCTION

1. *LAL*, p. 116.
2. Walter Hooper's phrase in a letter published in *LAL*, p. 120.
3. *TST*, p. 566.
4. *LL*, p. 308.
5. *LL*, 'Memoir' p. 25.
6. Sheldon Vanauken, *A Severe Mercy* (Hodder and Stoughton, 1977), pp. 108–9.
7. Vanauken, *ibid*, p. 84.
8. Vanauken, *ibid*, p. 90.
9. Vanauken, *ibid*, pp. 91–2.
10. Vanauken, *ibid*, p. 93–4.
11. Vanauken, *ibid*, p. 100.
12. Charles Colson, *Born Again* (Hodder and Stoughton, 1976).
13. Colson, *ibid*, p. 124.
14. See footnotes 1 and 4 above.
15. Martha Simmons, *A Guide through Narnia* (Hodder and Stoughton, 1979).
16. George Duncan, *Sustained by Joy* (Pickering and Inglis, 1981).
17. *LAL*, p. 117.
18. *LAL*, p. 115.
19. *LL*, p. 308.

Chapter Two A SKETCH OF LEWIS'S LIFE

1. *Light on C. S. Lewis*, edited by Jocelyn Gibb (Geoffrey Bles, London 1965), pp. 64–5.
2. *SBJ*, p. 11.
3. AEIC, pp. 7–8.
4. *SBJ*, pp. 15.
5. *SBJ*, pp. 222–3.
6. *TPR*, pp. 38–9.
7. See also page 27 in *SBJ*.
8. *SBJ*, pp. 31–2.
9. *TST*, p. 47.
10. *LL*, pp. 1–26.
11. *TST*, p. 53.
12. *LL*, pp. 32–3.
13. *LL*, p. 34.
14. *TST*, p. 180.

[15] *The Collected Poems of Wilfred Owen*, Edited by C. D. Lewis (Chatto and Windus, 1967), p. 55.
[16] Lewis, *ibid*, p. 44.
[17] *LL*, pp. 40–4.
[18] *TST*, p. 204.
[19] *TST*, p. 93.
[20] *TST*, pp. 115–6.
[21] *TST*, p. 19.
[22] *LL*, p. 101.
[23] *LL*, p. 103.
[24] *LL*, p. 107.
[25] *TST*, p. 301.
[26] *LL*, p. 108.
[27] Gibb, *ibid*, pp. 67–85.
[28] *C. S. Lewis Speaker and Teacher*, edited by Carolyn Keefe (Hodder and Stoughton, 1971), pp. 105–22.
[29] Gibb, *ibid*, pp. 44–5.
[30] Gibb, *ibid*, p. 65.
[31] Keefe, *ibid*, pp. 49–93.
[32] Humphrey Carpenter, *The Inklings: C. S. Lewis, J. R. R. Tolkien, Charles Williams and their friends* (Unwin Paperback, 1981).
[33] Carpenter, *ibid*, p. 226. But see also *Biog.*, p. 157.
[34] Vanauken, *ibid*, p. 109.
[35] *LAL*, p. 34.
[36] *SLE*, pp. 1–14.
[37] *Biog.*, p. 285.
[38] See last chapter, 'An Appraisal'.
[39] *LL*, p. 275.
[40] *Samson Agonistes*, edited by Ann Phillips (University Tutorial Press), p. 97.

Chapter Three VISIONARY AND ALLEGORIST

[1] David Daiches, *A Critical History of English Literature* (Secker and Warburg, revised edition, Landan 1969), volume 3, p. 586.
[2] This quotation and the two others printed above are taken from Roger Sturrock's edition of *Pilgrim's Progress* (Oxford University Press, 1966).
[3] Carpenter, *ibid*, p. 151.
[4] The issue of 12th July, 1974.
[5] *SBJ*, p. 189.
[6] *SBJ*, p. 196.
[7] *SBJ*, pp. 196–7.
[8] Taken from *The Oxford Book of Christian Verse*, chosen and edited by Lord David Cecil (Oxford University Press, 1965 edition), p. 510.
[9] *SBJ*, pp. 205–6.
[10] *SBJ*, p. 209.

[11] See Vanauken, *ibid*, p. 88.
[12] *SBJ*, p. 215.
[13] *SBJ*, p. 223.
[14] *TST*, p. 425.
[15] *TST*, p. 428.
[16] *TST*, p. 425.
[17] *TST*, pp. 353–4.
[18] *TST*, pp. 384–7.
[19] *TST*, pp. 385–6.
[20] *Biog.*, p. 128.
[21] *SLE*, p. 147.
[22] *TST*, p. 445.

Chapter Four: THE IMAGINATIVE APOLOGIST

[1] *CR*, p. 144.
[2] *Un.*, pp. 64–76.
[3] *Un.*, p. 65.
[4] *Un.*, p. 66.
[5] *Un.*, p. 67.
[6] *Un.*, p. 73.
[7] *Un.*, p. 76.
[8] *Un.*, p. 67.
[9] *AMA*, p. 127.
[10] *AMA*, p. 124.
[11] *Un.*, p. 68.
[12] *Un.*, pp. 70–2.
[13] *Un.*, pp. 283–4.
[14] *Un.*, pp. 212–3.
[15] *CR*, p. 129.
[16] *CR*, p. 129.
[17] Preface to *CR*, p. vii.
[18] Preface to *MC*, pp. 5–6.
[19] *MC*, pp. 6–7.
[20] Michael J. Christensen, *C. S. Lewis on Scripture* (Hodder and Stoughton, 1980), pp. 24–42.
[21] *MC*, p. 12.
[22] *UN.*, pp. 67–8.
[23] *P*, p. 129.
[24] *Biog.*, p. 248.
[25] *MC*, pp. 20–1.
[26] *MC*, p. 30.
[27] *MC*, p. 30.
[28] *MC*, p. 32.
[29] *MC*, p. 37.
[30] *MC*, p. 37.
[31] *MC*, pp. 41–2.

[32] *MC*, p. 48.
[33] *MC*, p. 49.
[34] *MC*, p. 80.
[35] *MC*, pp. 52–3.
[36] *MC*, p. 55.
[37] *MC*, p. 54.
[38] *MC*, p. 56.
[39] *MC*, pp. 78–79.
[40] *MC*, pp. 79–80.
[41] *MC*, p. 116.
[42] *MC*, p. 126.
[43] *MC*, p. 149.
[44] *MC*, p. 188.
[45] *MC*, p. 59.
[46] *MC*, p. 173.
[47] *TST*, pp. 514–15.
[48] *TSD*, p. 36.
[49] *TSD*, p. 38.
[50] *TSD*, p. 39.
[51] *TSD*, p. 40.
[52] *TSD*, p. 40.
[53] *TSD*, pp. 42–3.
[54] *TSL*, pp. 82–3.
[55] *LL*, p. 177.
[56] *AMA*, p. 179.
[57] Hooper, *Past Watchful Dragons* (Fount Paperbacks, 1980) p. 9.
[58] *LL*, p. 260.
[59] Hooper, *ibid*, pp. 111–12.
[60] *TLWW*, p. 45.
[61] Printed at the back of the edition of *TLWW* used for the chapter.
[62] *TPR*, p. 149.
[63] *TPR*, pp. 149–52.
[64] *TPR*, p. 150.
[65] *TPR*, pp. 150–51.
[66] *CR*, pp. 152–66.
[67] *FS*, pp. 104–25.
[68] *FS*, p. 109.
[69] *FS*, pp. 109–11.
[70] *FS*, pp. 111–12.
[71] *FS*, pp. 112–13.
[72] *FS*, p. 113.
[73] *FS*, pp. 113–14.
[74] *FS*, pp. 114–15.
[75] *FS*, p. 125.
[76] *FS*, pp. 105–6.
[77] *Light on C. S. Lewis*, ed. J. Gibb, (Geoffrey Bles, London 1965).
[78] Quotations are from Eliot's *Collected Poems 1909–62* (Faber and Faber, London 1963), pp. 189–223.

[79] See also R. L. Purtill, *C. S. Lewis's Case for the Christian Faith* (Harper & Row, 1985).

Chapter 5: SCIENCE FICTION TOO

[1] *The New Encyclopaedia Britannica* (15th edition, Volume 8), p. 84.
[2] I have used the 1952 (Pan Books) edition.
[3] *OTSP*, pp. 21–2.
[4] *OTSP*, pp. 25.
[5] *OTSP*, p. 118.
[6] *OTSP*, p. 121.
[7] *OTSP*, p. 126.
[8] *OTSP*, p. 129.
[9] *OTSP*, p. 148.
[10] *Biog*, p. 162.
[11] *TST*, p. 492.
[12] *LL*, p. 195.
[13] *Biog*, p. 172.
[14] *Pet*, p. 49.
[15] See WL White, *Images of Man in C. S. Lewis* (Hodder and Stoughton, 1970), pp. 26–7.
[16] *AMA*, p. 80.
[17] Preface to *THS*.
[18] *THS*, p. 8.
[19] *The Abolition of Man*, p. 36.
[20] Talks broadcast on BBC Radio.

Chapter Six: LETTER-WRITER EXTRAORDINARY

[1] Twenty six of his letters (some are extracts) to Sheldon Vanauken have been published in *A Severe Mercy* (Hodder and Stoughton, 1977).
[2] The notes to this chapter use the abbreviations as in other chapters: LL–*The Letters of C. S. Lewis*; LAL–*Letters To An American Lady*; TST–*They Stand Together*.
[3] *TST*, pp. 565–6.
[4] *TST*, p. 106.
[5] *TST*, p. 534.
[6] *TST*, p. 540.
[7] *LL*, p. 142.
[8] *LL*, p. 291.
[9] *LL*, p. 291.
[10] See also *LL*, p. 158.
[11] *LL*, pp. 291–2.
[12] *see LL*, pp. 276–7.
[13] *LAL*, p. 40.
[14] *LL*, pp. 298–9.
[15] See *LL*, p. 202.
[16] See LL, p. 199.

[17] See *LL*, p. 256.
[18] *LL*, p. 217.
[19] *LAL*, p. 21.
[20] *LAL*, pp. 70–1.
[21] *LL*, pp. 289–90.
[22] *LL*, p. 262.
[23] *LL*, p. 250.
[24] *LL*, pp. 251–2.
[25] *LL*, p. 253.
[26] *TAFP*, pp. 26–50.
[27] *LL*, p. 286–7.
[28] See Christensen, *C. S. Lewis on Scripture* (Hodder and Stoughton, 1979).
[29] Francis Schaeffer, *No Final Conflict* (Downers Grove: Inter-Varsity Press, 1975).
[30] Harold Lindsell, *The Battle for the Bible* (Grand Rapids, Zondervan Publishing House, 1976).
[31] J. I. Packer, *Fundamentalism and the Word of God* (Inter-Varsity Fellowship, rep. 1963), pp. 95–6.
[32] *LL*, p. 251.
[33] *LL*, pp. 127.
[34] *LL*, p. 155–6.
[35] *LL*, p. 188.
[36] *LL*, p. 261.
[37] *LL*, p. 273.
[38] *LL*, p. 295.
[39] See *TST*, pp. 19, 21, 26, 354, 385, 428, 444–7, 449, 452–4, 467–8, 474–5.
[40] *LL*, p. 261.
[41] Preface to *LAL*, p. 5.

Chapter Seven: AN APPRAISAL

[1] *LL*, p. 285.
[2] *LL*, p. 92.
[3] *Biog*, p. 56.
[4] Carpenter, *The Inklings*, pp. 8–16.
[5] The phrase is from Hooper's edition of *TST*, pp. 535–8.
[6] Carpenter, *J.R.R. Tolkien: A Biography* (George Allen and Unwin, 1977), pp. 235–246.
[7,8] Carpenter, *J.R.R. Tolkien: A Biography* (George Allen and Unwin, 1977), p. 237.
[8] Gibb, *ibid*, p. 63.
[10] *LAL*, p. 89.
[11] *AGO*, p. 16.
[12] *AGO*, p. 11.
[13] *AGO*, p. 19.
[14] AGO, p. 18.
[15] *AGO*, p. 23.

16 *AGO*, p. 11.
17 *AGO*, p. 21.
18 *LAL*, p. 89.
19 *LAL*, p. 89.
20 *AGO*, p. 37.
21 *AGO*, p. 42.
22 *AGO*, p. 43.
23 *AGO*, p. 44.
24 *AGO*, p. 47.
25 *LL*, p. 127.
26 Gibb, *ibid*, p. 65.
27 Gibb, *ibid*, p. 65.
28 *Biog.*, p. 135.
29 *Biog.*, p. 134.
30 *LL*, p. 206.
31 See *Milton Criticism*, edited by James Thorpe (Routledge and Kegan Paul, 1965: paperback).
32 Thorpe, *ibid*, p. 354.
33 Thorpe, *ibid*, p. 370.
34 See introduction to Thorpe, *ibid*, p. 18.
35 From *Milton* (1947), published in *The Proceedings of the British Academy*, volume xxxiii.
36 See Thorpe, *ibid*, p. 314.
37 See Patrick Murray, *Milton: The Modern Phase* (Longmans, 1967), p. 1.
38 See F. R. Leavis, *Revaluation: Tradition and Development In English Poetry* (Chatto and Windus, 1969), pp. 43–4.
39 *A Preface to Paradise Lost* (OUP, 1943), p. 45.
40 Christopher Ricks, *Milton's Grand Style* (Clarendon Press, Oxford, 1963), p. 148.
42 *The Restitution of Man: C. S. Lewis and the Case Against Scientism* (Eerdmans, 1983), p. 65.
43 *Biog.*, p. 283.
44 *OHEL*, p. 393.
45 *Letters to Malcolm: Chiefly on Prayer* (Fontana Books, 1966), Chapter 6.
46 'Christianity and Culture', in *CR*, pp. 12–16.
47 Vanauken, *ibid*, p. 109.
48 *TAFP*, p. 203.
49 Michael Aeschliman, *The Restitution of Man: C S Lewis and the Case Against Scientism*, p. 3.
50 *Biog.*, p. 229.

Index